Culture
from the Inside Out

TRAVEL—AND MEET YOURSELF

Alan Cornes

INTERCULTURAL PRESS
A Nicholas Brealey Company

First published by Intercultural Press, a Nicholas Brealey Company.
For information contact:

Intercultural Press, Inc.
PO Box 700
Yarmouth, Maine 04096 USA
Tel: 207-846-5168
Fax: 207-846-5181
www.interculturalpress.com

Nicholas Brealey Publishing
3–5 Spafield Street
London, EC1R 4QB, UK
Tel: +44-(0)-207-239-0360
Fax: +44-(0)-207-239-0370
www.nbrealey-books.com

© 2004 by Alan Cornes

Printed in the United States of America

08 07 06 05 04   1 2 3 4 5

ISBN: 1-931930-04-X

Library of Congress Cataloging-in-Publication Data

Cornes, Alan.
    Culture from the inside out : travel—and meet yourself / Alan Cornes.
        p. cm.
    Includes bibliographical references and index.
    ISBN 1-931930-04-X
  1. Intercultural communication. 2. Cultural awareness. 3. Visitors, Foreign.
    I. Title.
    HM1211.C67 2004
    303.48'2—dc22

                                                                    2004005453

Contents

List of Figures

Acknowledgments

I would like to express my indebtedness to the many people who have made it possible for me to write this book. Some I have known for years; others I met only briefly and in passing.

In particular I would like thank both Toby Frank and Judy Carl-Hendrick for their support and guidance. Without Toby's initial interest in and commitment to my manuscript and Judy's perceptive and skillful recommendation for a logical structure, along with a multitude of useful suggestions, I am not sure whether this book would have ever been finished at all.

In the book I have inevitably drawn heavily, and with gratitude, on the work of experts across many fields, and the names in the References bear testimony to this.

I have also been guided by friends abroad who I am sure must have suffered many times from my cultural gaffes and lack of understanding.

Thanks also to those I have met on my travels. I have often been amazed and humbled by their generosity. Whether I was given a place to stay or food to eat, their hospitality was sometimes more than they could afford, but no payment was requested, and when offered, usually none was accepted.

Finally, I want to acknowledge my family and friends. The writing of this book, or at least my talking about it, has probably tried their patience numerous times; my apologies to you all.

Introduction

The writing of this book has been on the back burner for a number of years. The problem was that I was always able to come up with something else to do instead of writing, and traveling was often an excuse. "More research," I told myself, and of course I was right.

This book is based on my own and others' experience of what makes a good cross-cultural sojourner. The term *sojourner* has been used interchangeably with the term *traveler* throughout this book, and the reader should assume that both words have essentially the same meaning. In the same way, to avoid using formulas such as he/she, him/her, or his/her, I have simply alternated between genders throughout the book. The reader can assume that the person I am referring to can be either a man or a woman.

Other books have covered the theme of cross-cultural differences. Writers such as Geert Hofstede, Fons Trompenaars, Terence Brake, and Edward T. Hall have given the world some useful models to help us understand cultural differences. Fons Trompenaars (1997), in the second edition of his book *Riding the Waves of Culture,* offers approaches to help the reader manage or reconcile dilemmas arising from cultural differences.

Conceptual frameworks can certainly help the sojourner to make an informed guess as to what underlying values may be driving the behavior he is witnessing. As someone who has run a number of cross-cultural training programs, I have found that many participants do not know how best to apply their new knowledge in cross-cultural encounters. Just understanding about dimensions of cultural differences did not explain why some of their colleagues were clearly more effective at crossing cultural boundaries than others. What made the difference? The individual. The focus of this book is therefore on you, the person interacting cross-culturally. For some of you this approach may confirm what you already sense intuitively; for others it will provide personal insights and heightened self-awareness; and yet for still others, especially those who follow the reflections and exercises I have included, the effect may be purgative and possibly uncomfortable.

How do I define a successful cross-cultural experience? For the purpose of this book, I use a three-part analysis adapted from the work of Brent Ruben and Daniel Kealey (1979):

1. The sojourner feels comfortable and at ease in the new environment.
2. The sojourner is able to operate and to successfully complete tasks and projects.
3. Members of the host culture feel comfortable with the sojourner and enjoy his or her company.

This book aims to look at cross-cultural effectiveness from a different perspective. Specifically, what are the key differentiators between successful and less successful sojourners? Is the difference one of attitude, or is the effective culture crosser using a set of highly developed skills? What is the difference between the two? If the latter, what skills are involved? Can descriptive labels be found for what must often be a subjective insight or unconscious intuition? And, finally, can the less successful sojourner become more effective by learning new skills and approaches?

The competency frameworks adopted by many large organizations describe the knowledge, skills, and behavior required to carry out tasks but often without addressing the attitude, traits, values, beliefs, and underlying assumptions that drive employee behavior. Competency frameworks also sometimes confuse personality traits with skills and knowledge. For example, I have seen a competency framework in which *resilience* is described, among other things, as "an ability to be positive and to be able to maintain an optimistic outlook." If we take *ability* to mean "the power or capacity to be able to do something," in this case, maintain an optimistic outlook, then this seems to me to be more of a personality trait than a skill.

To make sense of such confusions, one first has to understand what is meant by knowledge, skills, and traits and how they are different. It is then possible for individuals who have some understanding of themselves to strengthen those areas that can be strengthened and to learn how best to operate with the talents and traits they have been given.

This book will provide you with questions, tools, and models that will help you explore and understand your own *thoughts, feelings, and emotions* in a more structured way. It will also help you to "learn from the inside" your emotional response to cross-cultural interactions and enable you to broaden your thinking so you should be better able to tackle the dilemmas you will undoubtedly meet.

If you struggle in the area of cross-cultural interaction and feel that you do not have a natural aptitude for it, this book should help you identify the areas you need to strengthen. Then you can better decide what knowledge and skills you can develop in order to compensate for any perceived blind spots. Simply knowing what is required may also help you to use your existing knowledge, skills, and traits to creatively negotiate cross-cultural situations.

In addition to building on the traits and skills you already possess, whether you are gifted in this field or not, you can improve your effectiveness by increasing your sensory acuity, empathy, and perceptiveness. You can work at reflecting on your interactions with others. To be effective, you also need to be aware of, acknowledge, and challenge your existing cultural baggage, beliefs, and prejudices.

Finally, there is one necessary addition to the qualities already mentioned: intent, integrity, sincerity, honesty, authenticity—call it by whatever label you choose, but without it you risk having only superficial success in building relationships. You may even leave those you meet with a sense that they have been "psychologically mugged" by someone who, though charming, was insincere and deep down did not really care about them. This "authenticity" must be distinguished from the notion that just being one's self is enough to ensure successful cross-cultural interactions. It is ethnocentric to think that everyone else should be able to understand you. Such a position is based on the assumption that your own culture and worldview is shared by everyone else.

The authenticity I am referring to is the genuine intention to connect with, and to build personal relationships with your hosts. This inevitably requires gaining an understanding and experience of the host's culture. This is different from gaining cultural understanding and experience simply in order to leverage cultural differences for organizational or economic reasons, or to utilize cultural diversity to build synergistic high performing teams. There is nothing wrong with these last two reasons but they are different in intent from the first. Your intent is often more obvious to others than you would think and what people read as your intent will affect how they judge your behavior. If your hosts approve of your intent, then they are more likely to forgive you when you fall short of local standards of social etiquette. I recall a man who, when preparing for a posting abroad, was told repeatedly that he must not under any circumstances lose his temper and openly show anger; to do so, he was told, would be considered the ultimate cultural faux pas in his new home. For six months he managed to present a calm and impassive face to his new work colleagues until one exceptionally stressful day an overload of work and misfortune caused him to lose his self-control and fire off a blast of angry words toward no one in particular. He returned to his office convinced that his outburst had condemned him to be a social outcast for the rest of his posting.

He was mistaken. Some of his colleagues asked solicitously if he was okay. Another confided that he was relieved to see that the visitor was not the unemotional "iceman" he had first appeared to be. One even said that she was glad that at long last he was starting to behave like a real manager. He felt he had crossed a Rubicon and relations with his colleagues continued to develop and improve from then on. He may have failed to meet the local standards of behavior but at least he had tried and his failure was not through a lack of intent but through being human. His lapse provided his colleagues with the beginnings of a new understanding into his character and for him, a new insight into his work colleagues and hosts.

Part I deals with feeling and emotions. You will be prompted to challenge some of your existing beliefs, particularly those that are unfounded and unlikely to serve you well in cross-cultural situations.

Part II explores what knowledge, models, and frameworks, coupled with your existing experience, can be valuable in helping you to analyze, prepare for, and meet the challenges that you are likely to face as you cross cultural boundaries. Part II also contains chapters aimed specifically at those who will be living in another culture or taking an extended visit abroad, though the material should also be of interest to those who are planning shorter trips or who will themselves be hosts to visitors from another country.

If you have no desire to connect with those from other cultures at any level deeper than the minimum required to get by, then put this book down; it is not meant for you.

PART I

Looking In

Look in the Mirror:
Who Are You?

Several years ago I worked overseas as a development volunteer in Kenya. During my stay I came into contact with many other volunteers as well as many expatriates, some of whom had lived and worked successfully in many other countries before arriving in Kenya.

I began to notice how some of them integrated easily into the host culture while others remained separate, even alienated, from it. At first I assumed that the secret must be personality or attitude. If a person was arrogant, rude, condescending, or racist, it was no great surprise to find that the local population (along with the expats and volunteers) did not enjoy his or her company.

I was soon forced to revisit this simplistic explanation when I encountered individuals who were generally liked by other expatriates and volunteers and who exhibited none of the aforementioned unpleasant qualities—but who were clearly not connecting with the host culture at anything other than the most superficial level. These people were quiet, understated, modest, sociable, and caring; my explanation clearly needed extensive revision. Perhaps, I thought, they did want to go any deeper. Was motivation the issue then? Sure enough, however, I soon came across examples of motivated people who wanted desperately to integrate more deeply but struggled in vain to break through the glass barrier.

Skills, Knowledge, and Traits

I observed these people in action as they communicated with the local population. I could not put my finger on anything specific that would have enabled me to say, "This is where you are going wrong." I suspected, even as I watched, that we were all missing the clues and instructions the hosts were conveying as to what was expected of us as guests in their country. In addition, maybe we were sending out unintentional nonverbal messages that contradicted whatever verbal message we were trying to communicate. I began to understand that effective cross-cultural interaction is an amalgam of knowledge, skills, and inherent traits, and I compiled the following list of competencies.

1. *A genuine desire to understand and connect with the host population*— a sincere, unambiguous curiosity coupled with a positive intent
2. *Self-knowledge*—a knowledge of one's strengths and blind spots especially with regard to interpersonal communication
3. *Self-assurance and control*—confidence and self-esteem
4. *Sensory acuity*—the ability to notice fine distinctions in the sensory information one receives
5. *The ability to empathize with another's viewpoint*—the desire to understand another's view of the world
6. *Emotional perceptiveness*—an awareness of one's own and others' emotional states
7. *Behavioral flexibility*—the ability to vary behavior to meet different situations
8. *A nonjudgmental outlook*—the ability to observe different values and behaviors impartially
9. *Humility*—a realistic appreciation of one's weaknesses and shortcomings
10. *Introspective reflection*—the ability to review and learn from experience

First, you must have a desire to connect. Next, the first impression you make must be positive, or at least neutral, so you must be aware of nonverbal messages and be able to control your own emotional state. You must be able to read subtle nuances of behavior in the cultural "other" and use that information to build rapport and to intuit what behaviors might be positively received or be inappropriate. To be able to do this, you must listen with the intent of understanding the situation from the other person's frame of reference. This is quite different from the techniques of active and reflective listening, where listeners show their attentiveness through their body language and by reflecting back what the speaker has just said. Next, you must be perceptive enough to note the subtle nonverbal responses you are receiving and be flexible enough to modify personal behavior accordingly. The attitude and spirit that support this should be one of nonjudgmental curiosity. You should have enough humility to be open to influence and even to accept personal limitations of logic, common sense, and cultural programming. You also need enough self-assurance to admit when you don't have a clue about what is going on and be comfortable with that admission. Finally, your curiosity should lead to later reflection on experiences and encounters as you try to make sense of them. Figure 1-1 shows the steps in the cross-cultural interaction process.

Later, when I returned to Britain, I researched what competencies others considered prerequisites for the successful crossing of cultural boundaries (see the Appendix). It soon became apparent that many of the qualities and competencies identified by the different surveys were similar and generally supported my own thoughts on the subject. However, the information still seemed incomplete, a bit like someone trying to learn tennis and being told that good tennis players should be fast, agile, and fit, with good hand and eye

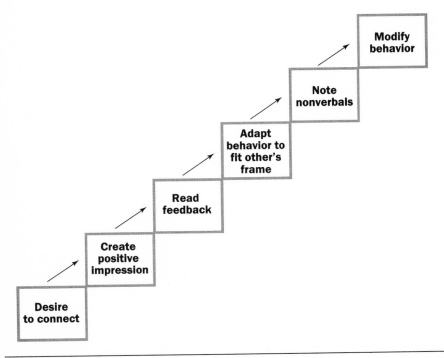

Figure 1-1   The Cross-Cultural Interaction Process

coordination, and also be talented tacticians. The learner is likely more interested in knowing where she stands in terms of ability and capability, to what extent she can improve, and what she needs to do to improve. In other words, she needs to practice to build her skill levels.

Another question was also unresolved: if an individual can develop these competencies, why, given equal training, were some individuals always clearly better at the task than others?

I realized that to have a chance of answering these questions, I first had to establish the differences among skills, knowledge, and personality traits and the extent to which each of these three can be learned or developed.

Skills

A skill is the *ability to do something well*. Words such as *expert, dexterous, adept,* and *proficient* are often used to describe how a skill is carried out.

Skills can be transferred from person to person. They are usually acquired by repeated practice and sometimes by breaking down the task into smaller, more manageable steps that enable one to gradually gain expertise with the whole. For example, a person might learn to use a map and compass to more skillfully navigate in unfamiliar locations, or become proficient at planning and organizing the logistical aspects of travel so that journeys run smoothly, despite unexpected (though ubiquitous) setbacks.

Knowledge

A person's knowledge is simply *all that one is aware of,* whether based on facts or experience.

Factual knowledge is information that can be taught; for example, the alphabet, the history of a country, how to wire a plug, and so on. Information about another culture's values, behaviors, and etiquette is knowledge that can be learned, even without traveling to the country itself.

Experiential knowledge, on the other hand, is composed of the understandings you accumulate as you progress through life. Such knowledge by definition is difficult to teach and is usually acquired firsthand. For example, when you reflect on an experience and realize that it correlates with a previous experience, what happened in the earlier instance may guide your response to the current situation. Acquiring experiential knowledge is really about reflection, about noticing patterns and connections with previous events and experiences, and assigning meaning to them. Responsibility for experiential learning is in the hands of the learner, because it is the learner who decides what is important, what to pursue, and what to learn more about. Over time we all come to understandings about ourselves and the values that guide our choices throughout life, and this is also a form of experiential knowledge. Knowledge can change over time as new experiences refine and build on past experience.

Travel, even encounters with groups or individuals within your own culture, often presents situations that fall outside of your previous experiences; the patterns just don't fit familiar templates. What you learn in such circumstances is again up to you. This is a crucial point to bear in mind if you want to learn more about another culture. In Chapter 3, I will suggest a strategy to help you become more systematic in capturing useful knowledge from your own cross-cultural experiences.

Traits

A trait may be described as a distinguishing quality of a person's character.

How traits are formed is still being debated. Usually the discussion revolves around the nature-nurture debate of whether a person's character development is driven more by genetic inheritance or by the environment and the way in which the child was raised. Whatever the cause, during the formative years each person will carve out a unique set of character traits, which makes each person a unique individual.

Regrouping the Ten Competencies

Taking the definitions of *skills, knowledge,* and *traits,* I then went back to my original list of ten competencies and attempted to group them under the three categories. This proved more difficult and thought provoking than I had anticipated. I classed a number of competencies immediately as traits but then realized that with motivation, even a person who apparently lacked certain traits or exhibited them only rarely could still improve her current position and acquire more of the competency she lacked. Some of the competencies can therefore fall under more than one grouping. For example, self-knowledge should clearly fall under "knowledge," but to consciously acquire it probably requires a willingness to do so. With all the possible overlapping in mind, I tentatively grouped my list as follows. This grouping is by no means scientifically conclusive—in fact, I recommend that you regroup the categories as you see fit. The exercise will help you think through the meaning of each competency.

Competence	Skill	Knowledge	Trait
A genuine desire to connect			•
Self-knowledge		•	
Self-assurance and control		•	•
Sensory acuity	•		•
Ability to empathize	•		•
Emotional perceptiveness	•		•
Flexibility			•
Nonjudgmental outlook			•
Humility			•
Introspective reflection	•	•	•

Skills, Knowledge, and Traits—A Summary

So far I have offered a list of ten competencies that correlate well with other existing lists of cross-cultural competencies. I have also defined the three most relevant terms—*skills, knowledge,* and *traits*—and attempted to group my original list under the definitions.

An important distinction is apparent from these definitions: Knowledge and skills can easily be taught or learned. Traits, however, are formed by a combination of factors: genetic inheritance, the way one is raised, and one's life experience. Traits are unique to each person and are not easily changed. Everyone has an individual combination of traits that creates recurring patterns of behavior. No matter how much we might want to be different, these traits tend to remain stable and familiar throughout our lives. Our traits are usually also our natural talents; they are what we are good at, our strengths, what we enjoy doing. They provide us with a source of satisfaction. Identify them and you will have made a good start toward seeing how they help or hinder intercultural encounters.

We now have an explanation of why, out of a group of people with roughly equal intelligence, experience, and knowledge of a particular culture, some people naturally fare better than others in cross-cultural situations. Just as some people are more practical, better with mechanical devices, or more organized than others, why shouldn't exceptional effectiveness in cross-cultural encounters also result from a particular set of inherent traits?

A study by Noreen Novick (Allport 1979, 435–36) supports this view. Some foreign students in a training school in the United States were asked to identify which of their fellow American students would be the most successful if posted by the U.S. Foreign Service to their country. The foreign students, though themselves from several different countries, were remarkably consistent in their choices of whom they considered would be welcome in their country; they were also equally consistent regarding those who would not be welcome at all. The investigator then searched for differentiating characteristics between those students everyone chose and those whom no one chose. They identified the crucial factor as "empathic ability." Those selected were perceived as being able to put themselves in other people's shoes and to size up, and be sensitive to, another's frame of mind. Those who were never selected lacked this ability.

This research highlights two important points:

1. An appreciation of skill in human relations is not specific to a given culture; all the nations represented chose the same gifted individuals.
2. The quality that was appreciated was a flexible capacity to know the other person's state of mind and adapt to it.

Individuals who are confident of their empathic ability in sizing up others are less anxious when meeting new people. They can trust their ability to read the cues they receive and adjust their own behavior accordingly so that they can avoid unnecessary confrontations and unpleasantness and can build successful relationships. Those lacking this ability cannot trust their skill in dealing with others and so must remain on guard. They also cannot trust their ability to interpret subtle nuances that provide the unique insights to each interaction; instead they tend to fall back on a "one-size-fits-all" approach based on stereotyping rather than on the information they could have gathered during the interaction.

Later in the book I will describe the Myers-Briggs Type Indicator,* a psychometric tool that can help you identify and understand your unique preferences and behavior, where you focus your attention, how you are energized, your preferences for taking in information and making decisions, and how you prefer to structure and live your life. I will also explain how all the characteristics, even those not apparently linked to the cross-cultural competencies identified so far, can be useful in different cross-cultural contexts.

---

*MBTI and Myers-Briggs Type Indicator are registered trademarks of the Myers-Briggs Type Indicator Trust. OPP Limited is licensed to use the trademarks in Europe.

Travel—and Meet Yourself

From my experience as a trainer, the foremost expectation of many people who attend cross-cultural training courses is to learn more about a specific culture or about other cultures in general. It is, however, equally important that you have a conscious awareness that some of your own values and behaviors may be specific to your own culture and determine the impact, both positive and negative, that you may have on those from different cultures. Without this awareness the study of other cultures lacks context and meaning. In a survey carried out by Kevin Barham and Marion Devine of the Ashridge Management Centre (see the Appendix), companies were asked to identify the most important characteristics needed by international managers. The significance of their replies is that, in contrast to the relatively lower priority assigned to "hard" or functional skills, four of the top six characteristics were "soft" skills, emphasizing the importance of human qualities involved in managing people from other cultures and the manager's ability to handle unfamiliar situations. However, one surprising and disheartening aspect of this survey is that only 2 percent of respondents ranked awareness of one's own cultural background as being among the five most important characteristics. Said differently, these international managers rated *an awareness of their own culture as the least important international competence out of the list of thirteen.* Sensitivity to other cultures was rated third in the same list, which, if you think about it, presupposes a solid awareness of their own cultural background; otherwise, how would they know what was different?

This last point builds on what we already know about skills, knowledge, and traits and about the importance of self-knowledge—that is, knowing your preferences, tendencies, traits, and the gaps in your current knowledge (here, your awareness of your own culture and cultural programming). When we can place more of our own behavior in a cultural context, we are less likely to assume that our behavior is universal. Most of us at times moderate how we behave, what we say, and how we say it to people we know, for example, when breaking bad news, offering condolences, being firm or gentle, acting as a team player, and so on. If we are able to do this successfully, it is because we usually know what sort of response to expect and have a good idea of how our message, favorable or otherwise, will be perceived. In cross-cultural encounters, however, this is the very information that is often not known. Yet without this basic but intrinsic understanding and knowledge, our success in cross-cultural relationship building will at best be inconsistent and at worst, nonexistent.

It has been stated that a person cannot be truly aware of his own cultural programming until he has experienced being in another culture. Only then, it is argued, is his view of how the world should work challenged, and what he previously assumed was universal is exposed as parochial after all. If the person is alone, he may experience the feeling of complete isolation. He is forced to fall back on his inner resources. In truth, the first person you meet is yourself. Even so it is very tempting in such circumstances to resist introspection and continue to look outside at external factors and see them as being responsible for your current state as opposed to your perception of those external factors. Our perceptions are often shaped by what we believe we already know.

Our behavior toward another person is governed not only by the context and purpose of the interaction and how the other person responds to us, but also by the personal baggage we take into the meeting. We all bring with us the background and history of our country of origin. For example, a Brit visiting Africa is, whether she likes it or not, part of an economic/ historical/political system that includes colonialism and neocolonialism, slavery, imperialism, aid, trade, and debt. That system also includes the history of black people in Britain, their struggles, and how the majority of white people perceive them.

Expatriates and other sojourners are not outside these systems of international relations; they are affected by their own country's past history and its present role in the international system. They will also be influenced by their own individual position and access to power and resources.

One does not have to be from a different country, or have a different color skin, to be seen as an outsider. Exactly how an outsider is seen, and sees himself, depends upon the social and political context and where the individual fits into it. Class, age, gender, race, culture, and many other aspects will affect the individual's actual and perceived power, status, and confidence. Most people remain unaware of their own racial prejudice. From our earliest years we are conditioned: Our parents pass along their beliefs and prejudices, and many children's stories, nursery rhymes, and toys express racist beliefs. Much of our literature and art contains negative stereotypes, and many of the jokes that people hear, at least in Britain, are either racist, antiblack, anti-Irish, antiSemitic, or sexist and antimen, antiwomen, or anti-gay. There are even jokes about the disabled. Even among those people who neither tell such jokes nor laugh at them, few are prepared to actually make a stand to discourage them. Popular beliefs, usually supported by media stereotypes, are full of racial prejudice. This is not so surprising in Britain, given the racial myths that developed from and since the colonial period.

If you bring personal bias in the form of prejudice or racism to an encounter, you will inevitably influence the message being communicated. It therefore helps to obtain a wider appreciation of the current underlying issues of any country you are going to visit, along with any relevant histori-cal background. You should also check if there are any current links between your own nation and the host country and, if so, how the host nationals per-ceive those links. Responsible travelers are politically aware travelers.

Strategies for challenging negative stereotyping and racial prejudice within yourself will be dealt with in a later section.

Values

Values can be described as a set of abstract and general principles that guide behavior. Individual values are, in effect, judgments about what is right or wrong, good or bad. These can be shared by members of a group, be it gen-erational, professional, societal, or cultural. The members of a particular culture may, for example, value a direct style of communicating whereby people should be as explicit as possible so as to reduce any misinterpretation or misunderstanding. Consider the values in Figure 1-2 that could vary between individuals or cultures.

Your values may clash with the prevailing values of the society or culture in which you reside or are visiting. Cross-cultural travelers often find them-selves in this position. Try this interesting exercise. Rank your ten most important values from this list: freedom, equality, independence, honesty, security, hard work, cleanliness, politeness, community service, law and order, justice, control, social relations, status, respect, conformity, individu-ality, structure, loyalty, achievement, variety, health, family, spirituality, edu-cation, creativity, knowledge, experience. Keep this list at hand; it will help if you can refer to it later when you are reading about important values orien-tations for the sojourner in Part II.

Value		Contrasting Value
Hierarchical relationships promote stability in society.	←——→	Egalitarianism promotes fairness and justice in society.
People should learn to look after others.	←——→	People should learn to look after themselves.
Caring for children is a mother's role.	←——→	Caring for children is shared between mothers and fathers.
One's role brings respect.	←——→	Ability and experience earn respect.
It is important to focus on work and to progress in your career.	←——→	It is important to focus on the quality of your life. Work is a means of achieving this.
Before you speak, take into account how others will react to what you are about to say. Directness is not valued because it can cause loss of face.	←——→	It is always important to tell the truth and say what you mean as clearly as possible. Directness is respected and is seen as a sign of openness and honesty.

Figure 1-2   Examples of Contrasting Values

Are You Communicating with Congruence?

When you travel abroad, who is the person you should know best and have most control over? Clearly yourself. So far we have looked at skills, knowledge, and traits as they relate to key cultural competencies. There is one more personal element that is critical to effective cross-cultural communication—and that is communication itself, both verbal and nonverbal.

You must be aware of the messages you are transmitting as well as the messages you are receiving. For example, suppose someone asked you a question and you were not sure of the right answer. If you gave her an answer anyway, it is likely that the other person would pick up that bit of doubt in the delivery of your answer. Even if you tried to disguise your uncertainty, some incongruence in your message would likely leak through. You cannot avoid communicating; even immobility and silence send a strong message. If you are operating in a culture with a different language and communication is a problem, remember that research by Albert Mehrabian (1972) has shown that when we speak, the words count for only about 7 percent of the overall message. What people understand of your message is largely governed by the way you say it: thirty-eight percent is conveyed by the tone in which you deliver your message, and 55 percent of the message is body language. This and other similar research findings are well known by those involved in training, acting, advertising, and communication in its many forms. However, an important point is often omitted: Mehrabian was referring specifically to the communication of emotion, feelings, or attitudes. Straightforward statements of fact such as "Yes, it is Tuesday today" can hardly be analyzed using the same percentage breakdown.

Even taking this last point into consideration, you may find these percentages a little hard to believe if you have not come across them before. However, think back to the last time you spoke to a friend on the phone who said, "Everything is fine," but the way in which he said it led you to believe the opposite. Imagine a nervous new employee telling everyone she was settling in well and quite comfortable with everything, while her body posture and facial expression told a different story. Incongruency in these situations is the contrast between the words, tonality, and body language. If your tonality and body language are at odds with what you are saying, then the person or persons at the receiving end must choose which message they believe— your words (7 percent) or your tonality and body language (collectively, 93 percent). Clearly, most people will go for the 93 percent.

We are extremely good at noticing incongruence in face-to-face communication, though we may be less adept at guessing the reasons behind it. As a cross-cultural communicator, you should be aware of what stereotypes and prejudices you hold. If you hold a negative stereotype of the nationality of the person you are communicating with, it would be very difficult, if not impossible, to stop some of that bias from leaking out, even if you want to make a positive impression. Figure 1-3 shows that while the words are supplied by our conscious thoughts, the tonality and body language are generally supplied through our unconscious mind, driven by our feelings and emotions.

By now you are probably starting to appreciate how important it is to become culturally self-aware; indeed, the first person you meet in a cross-cultural interaction is yourself. Likewise, the person you have most control over is yourself. But because we are human, we often throw up obstacles that hinder our ability to make the most out of a cross-cultural experience. We will explore some of these barriers in Chapter 2.

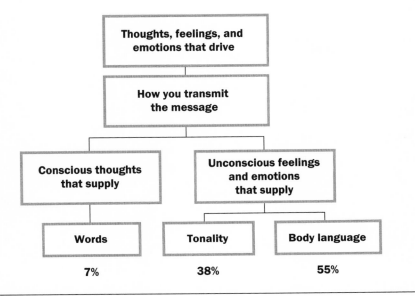

Figure 1-3   What Message Are You Communicating?

Self-Imposed Barriers

If you consider yourself a sociable person with good interpersonal skills then it is tempting to believe that learning more about the culture of the person you are about to meet is far more useful way of spending your time than gaining cultural self-awareness. Unfortunately this is rarely true, in fact both are important. Knowledge of another's culture is certainly useful if you are trying to see the world from their perspective, make the them feel more comfortable, or if you want to steer clear of committing embarrassing cultural gaffes. However, even if you are an acknowledged expert on the other's culture it still would be no guarantee that they would actually like being in your company. Other factors, that are more about who you are, as opposed to what you know, will determine this. This is why you need to be aware of some of the beliefs, assumptions, and ways of thinking that you hold that will influence your behavior and so have the potential to undermine and spoil your intercultural communications. Often we remain ignorant of these simply because they were acquired at an early age and were subsequently never challenged, especially if you never left your own culture. As a result when your intercultural relationship building does not go as well as you had hoped, you can be left with little idea of what went wrong. This chapter will look at six key barriers to the building of cross-cultural relations: (1) the wrong attitude, (2) deindividuation, (3) the misuse of stereotypes, (4) prejudice, (5) faulty beliefs, and (6) straitjacket thinking. It will also give you some strategies for overcoming them.

Your Attitude

How you relate to the host nationals is influenced by many factors. Your values, knowledge, skills, traits, the degree of incongruence you display when you communicate, the circumstances surrounding the interaction and your environment—all will affect how you relate to others in some way. The stress of adjustment combined with cross-cultural encounters can cause people to default to particular behaviors. However, the host nationals will almost certainly be unaware of the impact of these factors on you, or indeed, how you normally relate to people. *What they will see is your behavior and what they perceive as your attitude.* They will decide whether you are friendly, cooperative, interested, attentive, kind, generous, hostile, arrogant, impatient, evasive, defensive, naive, suspicious, remote, helpless, disinterested, or any other quality based on their experience of you.

Kenneth Clarke and George Miller (1970) describe an attitude as

> a disposition, acquired through previous experience, to react to certain things, people or events in particular ways. Attitudes represent a tendency to approach or avoid that which maintains or threatens the things one values. Like the values from which they are often derived, attitudes have an effect on and are consistently related to beliefs and behavior.

It seems reasonable to accept that an individual's attitude is derived from his values and reflects a tendency to react to certain events in certain ways. An individual's attitude will determine whether he approaches or avoids events that confirm or challenge his values, and it will also affect his behavior and beliefs. Is it possible to change a person's attitude? Yes, but only with great difficulty, the expenditure of much time and effort, and the use of sophisticated processes.

From the host's point of view, your attitude is simply what you project, what you reveal through your actions and behavior. The following model, Figure 2-1, explains the relationship between attitudes and behavior. Your attitude normally drives your behavior. The way in which your behavior is experienced by others can in turn influence their attitude and subsequently the way in which they behave toward you. The impact of their newly adjusted behavior may then influence your attitude, and so on.

It is, however, very easy to give people the wrong impression of yourself,

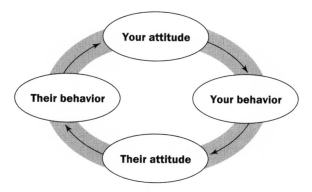

Figure 2-1   Attitudes and Behavior Cycle

or at least a different impression from the one you intend. To illustrate how attitude may be deduced incorrectly from behavior, I have taken the un-scientific approach of creating some fictitious and rather extreme carica-tures of sojourner types I have encountered over the years. Then, to add insult to injury, I have indulged in some amateur psychoanalysis of each. Read through the types and see if you recognize any of the behavior patterns and then work out what they all have in common.

Sojourner Types and Their Attitudes

THE WORLD-WEARY SOJOURNER. Laconic and unimpressed. "Been there, seen it, done it, got the T-shirt. It's nothing new."

Are such types really world-weary? Can all the richness and variety the world has to offer no longer stimulate their jaded palates? Experience in another country is not in itself an indicator of a person's ability to under-stand and integrate into another culture. If the World-Weary Sojourner is no longer impressed, perhaps it is because she has stopped noticing what is around her. An attitude of bored indifference may be an attempt to mini-mize or deny the cultural differences she does not want to address. An inner need to seize on, and always emphasize, the similarity between countries, cultures, people, and their basic values is often a traveler's attempt to sub-sume difference into a known and comfortable worldview. So is the world-weary attitude really a facade—an unconscious denial of any culture shock or discomfort, a refusal to admit she has reached the limit of her comfort zone and is maybe not as experienced as she wishes to appear? If so, then the cultural learning necessary to her integration will not take place, for why should she want to learn more if she knows it all already?

THE ADVISER. Paternal and superior. "Let me show you how we do it back home."

Often characterized by "us and them" thinking, such types promote the impression that they are bringing the torch of civilization from its birthplace—their own country. Often, the greater the perceived difference between their own and the new culture, the more negative the evaluation of the host culture.

Is the Adviser simply grasping at an opportunity to reinforce and emphasize his own worth, competence, and "superior" cultural norms? What is his intention? Is he really advising, coaching, or offering assistance when he points out how the local standards of competence are lacking in comparison with his own?

THE SARDONIC OLD HAND (OFTEN COUPLED WITH ELEMENTS OF THE WORLD-WEARY SOJOURNER). Sardonic and wise. "Let me tell you what they are really like; only last week, I . . ." "That reminds me of a time when I traveled in the rural district, I slept on a straw pallet. . . ."

The old hand is ever ready to dip into a bottomless barrel of anecdotes that always seem to reinforce the same, rather negative, view of the host nationals. Has she stopped noticing any of her host's positive aspects? Has she in fact decided that she knows as much as she needs to know about the culture and its people? She certainly knows enough to participate in some of the superficial daily aspects of the local culture, such as eating, and has a basic use of the language. To go deeper would require a paradigm shift; she would need to see the world through a different frame of reference—her host's. So is the Sardonic Old Hand really trying hard to project a self-image that increases a sense of self-worth while justifying her reluctance or inability to take that next step? Is she even hiding an underlying insecurity?

THE MULTILINGUAL INTERNATIONAL SOPHISTICATE. Smooth and urbane. "Watch and see how it should be done."

Theirs is an impressive performance spoiled by being more style than substance, especially as the performers are more often in "broadcast" than in "receive" mode. They often have difficulty in letting a situation "breathe" by just being silent. It usually takes many years to become fluent in a language, so those who appear to have a reasonable working command of a language are expected to have a corresponding understanding of what behavior is expected of them. In effect, gifted linguists may find that their language ability raises local expectations that they will also know how to behave appropriately, often more so than their less-fluent colleagues. As we have already seen, words represent only a part of the overall message. Being open to mood, context, shared silences, and atmosphere and knowing how, when, and in what manner the message should be delivered is just as crucial, if not more so, than simply knowing what words to use.

THE CONCERNED MISSIONARY. Compassionate and concerned; involved. "Stop enjoying yourself; there is so much work to do here."

Is the furrowed brow for the host nationals (who may not appreciate being cast as helpless victims waiting to be rescued), or is it for something else? A local villager once asked me this question about an expatriate whom the villagers had seldom seen smile: "If he is so unhappy here, then why did he come?" followed immediately by "And if he is so unhappy with us here, then why doesn't he go home?" The villager was not being ungrateful, just curious.

Concerned Missionary types make not just themselves uncomfortable, they may make people around them uncomfortable as well. They may create an atmosphere that almost defies the locals to build meaningful relationships with them. They often look upon the "natives" as naive children needing to be saved. In some cases the Concerned Missionary's genuine concern and sincerity eventually shines through. However, if a person has accepted a post abroad to escape something in her life back home, then the situation is different. People who travel to escape often fail to realize that the seeds of their unhappiness are usually within themselves, and to escape to somewhere new and exotic is no escape at all. Such issues are best dealt with at the source and preferably before boarding a plane.

THE STREETWISE TOUGH NUT. Shrewd, belligerent, and distant. "You won't catch me with that one. Stuff your gift!"

Is the toughness real or is it just a front to keep the unfamiliar world at a safe distance? A belligerent or arrogant attitude is often used as a defensive shield. If a person is not confident of his interpersonal skills and his ability to read others' body language and assess whether their intent is benign or threatening, then he is more likely to approach situations with a defensive attitude. When combined with the additional factor of being in a strange culture, the defensive shield can be very large and impenetrable. So are tough-nut types really compensating for poor empathetic skills? Do they, in their anxiety, protect themselves from interactions that are more often life enhancing than life threatening?

I'M ALREADY A NATIVE. Smug local expert. "So you must be new here. Let me show you. . . ."

Adapting to life in a different country is not the same as actually integrating into another culture. Sometimes people confuse the two. "Going native" usually signals a deep-seated insecurity in a troubled identity, not a person who loves the new culture and wants to assimilate. The "native" often takes on the dress, the cuisine, and the mannerisms of the host national. But such behavior usually doesn't sit well with the locals, who view these types with suspicion.

Building genuine personal relationships with the hosts, developing a real understanding of the culture, and integration itself inevitably take time and motivation. Losing one's identity in the process, however, is not desirable.

PLEASE LIKE ME. Smiling, friendly, trusting, eager, and placatory. "I don't really know you, but of course I'll lend you the money. Yes, you're right of course."

Please Like Me is an "It's a Small World After All" type, relentlessly positive about the host culture. But is her optimism based on experience and a real depth of knowledge, or is it merely based on an idealistic "We're all the same" fantasy that will evaporate in the wake of the first crisis she encounters? Her sunny personality may even be replaced by bitter disillusionment and a retreat to negative stereotyping, a Sardonic Old Hand in the making.

Sometimes those trying to counter the threatening impact of cultural differences adopt a similar position. Instead of the more common approach of either denigrating the local culture or emphasizing the superiority of their own, some expatriates and sojourners hold up the host culture as being superior to all others and, in particular, their own. This is just another form of ethnocentrism, where the individual merely sees another culture as the center of everything. All other cultures, including her own, are then measured negatively against it.

THE AMATEUR ANTHROPOLOGIST. Informed, analytical, detached. "I find it fascinating the way in which they always. . . ."

Are the host nationals merely being studied like specimens in a laboratory, or does the observation extend into actually connecting, building relationships, and gaining understanding through personal experience? The Amateur Anthropologist is at least taking a nonjudgmental interest in the local population and culture. To progress further, however, he needs to develop communication skills that enable intercultural communication and cultivate the ability to empathize with the locals and their frame of reference. The essence of empathy is not that you agree with someone but that you understand that person (and, in this case, their culture) at a deep level emotionally as well as intellectually.

Is the Amateur Anthropologist ready, or able, to take that next step or does the detached, analytical attitude keep him closed off—and safe—from the scary prospect of becoming a vulnerable culture earner? Is his attitude a front so he can say, "Hey look, I am really interested in you and your culture" while at the same time maintaining his position as an outsider looking in, and therefore with no need to open himself to any emotional commitment?

THE CHARACTER (OFTEN COUPLED WITH ELEMENTS OF THE SARDONIC OLD HAND). Unashamed eccentric. "I've always been like that. If they don't like it, then tough!"

Was the Character really always like that back home? People often behave differently away from the social controls that inhibit them in their own culture. Behavior that they would not have gotten away with, nor had the courage to exhibit, back home in front of family, friends, and work colleagues can often blossom abroad, uninterrupted and unchallenged. Eventually, their eccentricity becomes their identity. The question they must ask themselves is, Does this behavior serve me well or is it just a self-indulgent prop to raise my own self-esteem while actually distancing me from people?

THE SELF-SUFFICIENT SOJOURNERS. A close couple, no assistance required. "What does the guidebook say about this town?"

In public they are often seen wearing headphones, engrossed in a guidebook or novel, or conversing closely with each other. Local knowledge, cultural insights, flora and fauna, good places to stay, good places to eat, things to see—all are thoroughly researched but tend to come from the Internet, the printed page, or from tips supplied by other expatriates rather than from their personal interactions with the host nationals. They are professional expatriates who are practiced at handling the logistical aspects of travel and adapting to a comfortable life quickly in a variety of new environments. They energetically seek out all the country has to offer in the way of scenery, wildlife, activities, and historical sites. They snorkel, bungee jump, and safari, and back home their travel experiences give them prestige and status.

They are happy to go anywhere, yet by choice, integrate nowhere. They are naturally outgoing, warm, and friendly, so it is not introversion that prevents them from integrating more, but a conscious decision not to do so. It is their pragmatic solution to the emotional upheaval they would face if they put down roots in every country they lived only to have to pull them up again when they move a year or two later. It is a solution that works well for them, and, despite their emotional detachment from the host nationals, they are invariably polite and friendly and make good hosts to those they invite into their home. Though this strategy may in fact be the best approach for these travelers, there is still a price to be paid. The locals who come into contact with them, though initially impressed by their friendly manner, soon come to realize that the self-sufficient sojourners are indiscriminately friendly to everyone they meet. They also sense that something is being held back in the sojourners' interactions, and that there is a line over which they are not expected to cross. The strategy of noninvolvement works for the Self-Sufficient Sojourners, but it inevitably has an impact on how they are perceived by the locals. Their emotional detachment effectively prevents relationships from developing further. Unaware of the logic behind their behavior, the locals may conclude that the Self-Sufficient Sojourners feel they are superior to them in some way. When the sojourners finally return home, they will have a room full of exotic artifacts and many exciting travel stories to tell, but few, if any, new friends to write back to.

So what was the common denominator? Did you spot it? In every case the attitude adopted was a front to conceal some concern, anxiety, or insecurity. There was a mismatch between the way individuals felt on the inside and how they expressed their feelings in language and behavior. Put simply, *they were not being themselves.* These caricatures illustrate how an attitude can be used as a shield to cover a perceived weakness and subsequently lead the traveler into unhelpful patterns of behavior. The unfortunate result of using this shield is that the ability to communicate with congruent verbal and nonverbal signals is undermined. Suppose in each of the above cases the character cast aside the front and interacted without pretense. For example, if a traveler felt nervous or insecure, she would acknowledge this fact, at least to herself, and possibly even to a close confidant. Would her effectiveness be enhanced or damaged? I suspect the former, since acceptance is always the first necessary step toward overcoming self-imposed barriers.

It seems only fitting that this section close with a description of a sojourner type that illustrates the attitude an effective visitor or expatriate should have.

THE RESPECTFUL AND CURIOUS GUEST. Comfortable, open-minded, relaxed, outer-directed, curious, respectful, and humble. "That's interesting, thanks for inviting me."

These travelers are clear about what they know and what they need to learn. They are aware of their own strengths and weak spots. However, their focus is more on their hosts than on themselves. These travelers prefer to let information emerge in the general course of events rather than subject people to a barrage of questions, though any questions asked will take account of the context and mood at the time. Also, they are not just gathering information; they are interested in understanding the world *from their host's perspective.* They want to learn and have a natural curiosity to try and understand other people. It is in their nature to want to make friends.

This attitude allows the traveler congruence with her perceived shortcomings. In listing humility as one of the desirable traits, I am not thinking of a Dickensian Uriah Heep sort of humbleness, but rather, a realistic appreciation of self. A traveler should be aware of her own strengths, weaknesses, and significance in the great scheme of things. An inflated sense of self-importance will create a barrier between the visitor and those who could actually assist her and help her learn; in short, it will get her nowhere.

I recall a story set in a busy airport. A flight is canceled and hundreds of people are affected. Some are despondent; many are angry. A queue of frustrated passengers builds up at the airline information desk, desperate for news of an alternative flight. One man storms past all the other travelers and forces his way to the front of the queue. "I demand that you put me on another flight immediately!" he shouts. A woman staffing the desk tries to placate him, but in reply he thumps his fist on the counter and roars, "Do you know who I am?" Calmly, the woman switches on the microphone of the airport speaker system and makes the following announcement: "There is a man here who does not know who he is; if you recognize him, please report to the information desk."

You don't need to be a psychotherapist to see that people waste a lot of energy trying to contain and conceal what in reality would not harm them if they acknowledged their frustration or insecurity. The following sections provide information that will allow you to challenge some of your own attitudes that may be inhibiting you and making you less effective.

Deindividuation

Some readers may be thinking that, far from becoming inhibited when travelling, for them the opposite is true—travel is an opportunity to cast off the stifling social constraints and inhibitions of their own culture. This is probably more common for travelers who are not intending to stay abroad for a long period. If no one is harmed or offended when travelers "let their hair down" and lose their inhibitions, then who has the right to stand in judgment? On the other hand, how many of us have been surprised, embarrassed, or even outraged by the thoughtless antics, attitudes, and more extreme behavior of our fellow countrymen, or -women when on holiday or business abroad?

Social psychologists use a term to describe what happens when people are no longer surrounded by family or community—entities that give them their status but also act as an effective censure of their behavior. The word is *deindividuation*. Closely intertwined with status is identity. The people who form an individual's circle of contacts also confirm the status upon which that person's identity may be built; for example, respected, professional, reliable, important, or senior. Once outside of this circle, the person is no longer recognized as having a particular status or identity. This in itself can be a major source of anxiety, especially for people whose public status forms a major part of their identity and self-worth. If they also suffer from low self-esteem and self-confidence, their anxiety will be even greater when their status is no longer continually reinforced by those around them. The fact that the hosts also do not accord them the respect they are accustomed to back home, and to which they feel they are entitled, rankles. One response to this loss of status is to revert to atypical behavior that would be seen as completely out of character by their usual circle of contacts. This process is deindividuation in a nutshell.

The concept of deindividuation was developed by Philip Zimbardo (1970), whose research showed the effect deindividuation could have on the behavior of individuals. In one experiment, Zimbardo arranged for cars to be abandoned in both big cities and smaller communities. The cars that had been abandoned in the big cities were quickly broken into and stripped of anything of value. The cars abandoned in the small communities, however, were left untouched. It is easy to be anonymous in a city since it is virtually impossible to form any real relationship with all the inhabitants. As a result, cities are seen as more deindividuating. Those vandalizing the abandoned cars were not concerned if others, whom they did not know and who did not know them, saw them breaking rules of normal behavior.

In contrast, if a local had vandalized one of the cars left in his own small community, first he would have been identified straightaway. But also, the community's view of the vandal's status would thereafter have been altered—downward. Urbanized society may offer more settings for people to become individuated than rural life, but travel to any destination where one is unknown has the potential to deindividuate that person.

Abroad, travelers are to a large extent anonymous, or deindividuated from their normal social group. They are also no longer censored, so there is little chance that they will damage their reputation or shock those they respect (unless they make the national news for some misdemeanor). In his travel book *The Old Patagonian Express* (1980, 85), Paul Theroux captures this freedom from restraint as he comments, "We were far from home; we could be anyone we wished. Travel offers great occasions to the amateur actor."

Travelers may also feel less pressure to control emotions that would normally be repressed. Moreover, they may be indifferent to, or fail to recognize, the standards of behavior in their new environment. Host nationals on the receiving end of the more aggressive sort of this behavior can only perceive it as ignorance or a lack of respect. In either case, any opportunity that the traveler may have had to integrate into normal sections of the new community will have disappeared.

You may have been annoyed by my caricatures and crude stereotyping. The following section looks specifically at the important area of stereotyping, why we stereotype, and the different forms it can take, both positive and negative.

Generalizations and Stereotypes

Generally speaking, stereotypes refer to categorizing people as a group while ignoring their individual differences. For example, when we say that Americans are naive, Arabs are irrational, Africans are lazy, Germans are uptight, or politicians are crooks, we are using stereotypes.

Everyone employs generalizations. We must group common elements together to form logical categories, or how else could we make sense of our world? We cannot respond individually to all of the isolated elements and people we encounter every day, so we group them into categories and then respond to the categories. Generalizing, in this respect, is inevitable. Stereotyping, however, is not. Although generalizing groups people together, it still allows for individual differences. If we generalize, for example, that New Yorkers are unfriendly, we still keep an open mind in case we meet a New Yorker who is friendly—which is in fact a common occurrence. A stereotype of New Yorkers as unfriendly pushes all New Yorkers into that category and ignores those who don't fit.

Robert Adler wrote an article titled "Pigeonholed" in the *New Scientist Journal* (2000, 38–41). In the article Adler recounts a story told by Deborah Best, a psychology professor at Wake Forest University in Winston-Salem, North Carolina. Best found her two nieces, aged three and five, playing together. One was pretending to be sick while the other one pretended to be a nurse looking after her. Best asked the niece playing the part of the nurse why she wasn't a doctor and was told, "Girls can't be doctors!" Even at that age, the girls had absorbed this stereotype, despite having an aunt who was a professor in psychology and despite the fact that they had been cared for since birth by a female doctor.

Best's studies of children have shown that many stereotypes sneak into our minds when we are too young to evaluate them. By the age of four, children can describe their culture's stereotypes of men and women, youth and age, ethnicity and race and can agree with stories that support these stereotypes. Another study by Lee Osterhout, M. Bersick, and J. McLaughlin (1977), measured electrical activity in adults' brains. The study revealed that when gender stereotypes were violated in sentences such as "The surgeon prepared herself for the operation," the level of electrical activity in the listener's brain surged in the same way it would in response to a sentence that makes no grammatical sense. Stereotypes clearly influence us all, far more than we would like to think.

Stereotyping will always be a factor that can influence cross-cultural effectiveness. A refusal to deal with stereotyping means a refusal to deal with one of the most basic aspects of thinking and communicating.

Generalizing not only helps us organize our thinking, it can also make more information available. For example, if you are going to meet a citizen from Japan, you will draw upon additional information relating to the Japanese in general, based on your current perception of the Japanese. You may predict that they will have dark hair and brown eyes, be courteous, polite, hardworking, speak English with a Japanese accent, and so forth. Such information can be useful, but it can also be dangerous, because the individual you meet may be completely different from what your stereotypical preconception led you to expect, and time and effort are consumed in overcoming the inappropriate image.

Generalizations and stereotypes are therefore part and parcel of how we think and are not automatically negative, as some people would have us believe (consider "East Asians are good students"). Generalizations and stereotypes tend to be held with the following understandings:

Generalizations	Stereotypes
• They are retained consciously.	• They are retained unconsciously.
• They are descriptive, not judgmental.	• They are judgmental, not descriptive.
• They are accurate.	• They may be accurate but are often not.
• They are considered a best first guess.	• They are the only consideration.
• They are modified by subsequent experience.	• They are not modified by experience.

All people use stereotypes, but some people are more aware than others that any stereotype should be open to modification. For some, the question is closed and the attributes included in their stereotypes are seen as completely defining the people within those categories. Clearly, if someone is serious about understanding people from another culture, holding a more open and modifiable view of stereotypes is necessary.

In addition to helping us organize our world, stereotyping can also fulfill more negative functions.

THEY PROVIDE SECURITY, SAFETY, AND REASSURANCE. The world is as you want it to be. You know where you belong; you know who your friends and enemies are. In short, you know what is what, and "strange" behaviors and customs you see abroad, though unusual and incomprehensible, do not impress you in the least. Your opinion is encapsulated in the stereotype, because that's where you got it from in the first place. So why gather any additional information and challenge what you are already comfortable with?

THEY SUPPORT AN INNER NEED. Stereotypes can support basic feelings of self-esteem and even a need to feel superior. If you believe that you have grown up in a society that practices "proper" behavior, then you can look down on other cultures (or social classes within your own culture) who do not meet your standards. Maybe your acceptance into one group is dependent upon your rejection of members of another group. People with low self-esteem or who are basically insecure are particularly prone to this sort of peer pressure.

THEY CONFIRM EXISTING AND LIFELONG BELIEFS. It has been said that children acquiring their first language learn more than a set of vocal skills; they take on the worldview of their group (Brown and Lenneberg 1965, 244–45). Many stereotypes are planted at an early age and remain unchallenged in adulthood. People tend to see what they expect or want to see. It is very easy to confirm a stereotype by selectively noticing that which supports it and ignoring that which undermines it. Taken a step further, if a person actively seeks information to support a given stereotype, he will tend to feel more confident in his belief; after all, he can always quote from his own "research."

THEY APPEAL TO SOME CHARACTER TYPES. To individuals with an oversimplified, rigid view of the world, stereotypes can offer the illusion of packaged certainty. Stereotypes provide security to such people because they can see the world through categories that they know and can handle. This, of course, is also an attractive option for individuals who are timid and insecure and feel threatened by opinions that conflict with theirs. For them, what is different is dangerous rather than interesting. In debates and arguments, the timid can always refer to the stereotype and hold it up as if it were universal truth. This is often referred to as *prejudicial stereotyping*. This type of stereotyping involves not only seeing everyone from a particular group as being the same, it also involves a negative judgment of that group. I will explore prejudice in more detail in the next section.

Prejudicial stereotyping is often part of the character makeup of "authoritarian" types, who hold a rigid, oversimplified view of the world. For example, those who hold extremely right-wing or left-wing views, who follow authority without question, and who in turn are not tolerant of criticism from their subordinates fall into this category. Such types can feel themselves superior to other groups on the basis of a group characteristic that in itself is insignificant (being white/male/American/a football supporter of a particular team). Such prejudices invariably reflect and say more about the person who holds them than the person or persons they are leveled at.

Yet another reason for consciously avoiding the use of negative stereotypes (not that any more are needed) is that recent research by Jeffrey Hausdorff of Israel Deaconess Medical Center in Boston and Becca Levy of Yale University (2000) has shown that being exposed to negative stereotypes can have a debilitating physical impact. For example, when elderly people were exposed to stereotypes—in the form of negative or positive "trigger" words—and then challenged with a series of math tests, those exposed to negative words became stressed. Their heart rate, blood pressure, and skin conductance all increased and stayed high for thirty minutes. Those exposed to positive cues sailed through the tests stress-free. In the same way, the researchers found that negative words could make the elderly walk more slowly and underrate their physical capability and even sap their will to live. Similar tests, only this time utilizing sexist television commercials, were carried out by Paul Davis of the University of Waterloo in Ontario (1999). He found that the advertisements affected the young female graduates in their ability to solve difficult math problems. Similar studies focusing on racial stereotyping have uncovered equally disturbing results. It seems that not only are the consequences of negative stereotyping more far-reaching than expected, but stereotyping itself is more pervasive than previously thought.

Because I have used the term *prejudice* in this section and because stereotyping and prejudice go hand in hand, I will define what I mean by the word.

Prejudice

Prejudice can be seen as the almost inevitable result of prejudicial stereotyping. It is negative judgment resulting in any attitude of extreme dislike or hatred toward a group of people based on the negative stereotypes that are perceived to be true of all members of the group. People hold certain prejudices because they do not want to admit uncomfortable things about themselves. The prejudice protects them from harsh reality. For example, someone who is unsuccessful in a business venture might protect himself from feeling like a failure by believing that others succeeded only by employing the dishonesty and deceit characteristic of their type. Unfair treatment of an individual or group because of a negative perception of the whole group to which he is seen to belong is called discrimination—or prejudice in action.

In his landmark book *The Nature of Prejudice* (1954), Gordon Allport gives a five-point scale to describe how prejudice can be expressed.

1. Extermination
2. Physical attack
3. Discrimination
4. Avoidance
5. Verbal rejection

The model is an ascending scale moving from one to five, with the implication that the final three levels can be avoided if sufficient attention is directed at the first two levels.

This last section may have appeared rather negative. We all hold stereotypes, and doing so does not typecast you as a hopeless bigot. What *is* important is that you are aware of the stereotypes you hold and why—particularly any prejudicial stereotypes—and have the will to amend them in the light of new knowledge and experience. In fact, rather than waiting for new evidence that might change your ideas, take a proactive approach—challenge the assumptions on which your stereotypes are based and see how much, if any, hard evidence supports them. This can be an uncomfortable process because it may raise questions that challenge your beliefs about the world and about yourself. Your readiness to do this, and the depth to which you go, is one of the indicators that separates those who are likely to communicate with congruity and integrate well with people from other cultures from those who are not.

Deconstructing Unwarranted Stereotypes

So how do you become aware that you are holding an unfounded stereotype, and how can you best challenge it? As we have seen, stereotypes are generalized categorizations that describe people; can you be more specific than that? Try producing two lists on any national group you feel you know something about, headed something like this:

Germans are	*Germans are not*

Your lists will probably include words that act as descriptive labels in the minds of those who read them as well as those to whom they are directed.

Words like *outgoing, parochial, workaholic, lazy, extrovert, reserved, honest, corrupt, clever, polite, open, devious,* and so on, when applied to an individual or group, tend to act as an all-embracing classification. In short, words that should be active, changing descriptions are used as fixed labels, or judgments, that are static and do not change over time. Such judgments can be challenged by turning the stereotype into a question; for example, take the stereotype "The English are lazy." Ask "What do the English do that makes them lazy?" followed by "Every single English person?" and then "Which English person specifically?"

Another way to spot and challenge unwarranted stereotypical statements is to look for presuppositions. A *presupposition,* a term taken from Neuro-Linguistic Programming, is an idea or belief that is taken for granted and acted upon as if it were true. Presuppositions are in effect the silent assumptions that form your model of the world. You are generally unaware of them. Presuppositions always exist in unfounded stereotypical statements; they refer to what has to exist as true for the rest of the statement to make sense. In order to flush out presuppositions from a statement, ask yourself what would have to be true for the statement to make sense.

For instance, let's examine the following statement: "Everybody knows that Germans have no sense of humor." Now ask yourself, What would have to exist as true for everyone to know that Germans have no sense of humor? This question reveals the presuppositions contained in the statement:

1. There exists a group of people categorized as "Germans."
2. These Germans have no sense of humor.
3. Everyone in the world knows all the Germans that exist.
4. There exists a set of criteria by which a sense of humor (or a lack of it) can be judged.

Having brought the propositions into the open, you can now challenge them by asking the following questions: What leads me to believe that? or How specifically do I know that? You can then see if your "silent assumptions" stand up to scrutiny.

Let's try another example: "You can never trust Africans because they always stand up for their friends." What would have to exist as true for that statement to be true?

1. There exists a group of people categorized as "Africans."
2. All of these Africans have friends.

3. They always stand up for their friends.

4. Because Africans stand up for their friends, you cannot trust them.

Now let's challenge these presuppositions. A good question to start off with could be one aimed at checking the linkage hinted at in presupposition 4: Is it okay to trust those Africans who do not stand up for their friends or who have no friends?

Presupposition 2 can be challenged with the question: How specifically do you know that all Africans have friends? By bringing the underlying presuppositions out in the open and then challenging them, the illogical and often absurd nature of a statement is quickly revealed.

Conversation Quality Control Check

Next time you are sitting with a group of friends relaxing and talking about nothing in particular, sit quietly for a moment or two and listen carefully to what your friends are actually saying. If you were to examine every sentence and weigh the words used and their meanings, you would probably find them littered with generalizations, some with bits of information missing and even some statements that literally make no logical sense at all. For example: "I came in and sat down and they were all waiting for me. The boss just nodded so I knew she was angry."

The speaker has eliminated the information she feels is irrelevant or superfluous to the story, such as where she came in from, why she came in, where exactly she sat down, who specifically was waiting for her, how many people were waiting for her, why were they waiting, and what connection existed between her boss nodding and her boss being angry.

You, the listener, are expected to know from the context what the missing detail is and to fill in the gaps yourself. Normally, this causes no obvious problem in communication, and unless you work in an environment or profession (e.g., as a lawyer, accountant, or surgeon) where it is crucial to use language precisely, then the same will be true of discussions at work. If this were not the case, every conversation would last for hours as speakers provided every possible piece of supporting information. Since this book is about learning culture, let me give you some snippets of dialogue I have heard while abroad:

- "They don't understand me."
- "They rejected me."

- "Communication here is really poor."
- "Japanese parts are always best."
- "She always complains."
- "I must complete this project in three months."
- "The locals do not like me."
- "When I explain the procedure, he gets confused; he doesn't like me."

Most of us hear sentences like this every day and take them in stride. Unless there is a specific reason to get precise information, it would probably seem obsessive to do otherwise. However, it is through this sort of incomplete, stereotyped, and lazy use of language that negative stereotyping is reinforced, particularly in cross-cultural settings. Stereotyping demeans the infinite variety of human life and provides the tinder that keeps racism and prejudice alight. Following are some of the questions that could be asked to challenge the preceding statements by recovering the missing detail, narrowing the scope of the generalization, and checking where suspect connections have been inferred.

Statement	*Challenge*
• They don't understand me.	• Who specifically doesn't understand you?
	• How do you know they do not understand you?
• They rejected me.	• Who rejected you?
	• How specifically did they reject you?
• Communication here is really poor.	• Who is communicating what to whom?
	• What makes the communication poor?
	• How would you like to communicate?
• Japanese parts are always best.	• Every single one? Which ones?
	• Why are they the best?
• She always complains.	• Always? Every time she speaks?
• I must complete this project in three months.	• What would happen if you didn't?
• The locals do not like me.	• How do you know?

- When I explain the procedure, he gets confused; he doesn't like me.

- Is there a connection between your talking and his getting confused?
- Have you ever felt confused when talking with someone you like?

In general conversation, to launch into such a barrage of precise questions would soon annoy those on the receiving end. However, as mentioned earlier, some circumstances merit the effort. Also, the preceding list gives just the basic challenge. From experience, I have found that people tend to be less annoyed and therefore less defensive and more open to the positive influence of such clarifying questions if you deliver them with a softer lead-in and a slight rising intonation at the end. For example:

"That's interesting. How specifically did they reject you?"

"I was wondering, who specifically doesn't understand you?"

"I am curious. You say the locals don't like you? How do you know?"

In summary, to the extent you can, develop an internal quality control check on the information you are exposed to every day and tend to take in without question. You will be amazed at the result, and the practice will stand you in good stead for interacting in a different culture, when it is even more important that you are aware of your own use of language. In a different cultural context, whether abroad or in your own country, sensitivity to what you say and the way that you say it is likely to vary. The same words can have a different meaning and connotation in different cultural contexts and when different people hear them. In Britain if someone exclaimed, "Don't be stupid!" it would be taken as a rather harsh reprimand or admonition. In a country with a history of colonial rule under the British, the same exclamation coming from a British national might be perceived not only as a direct personal insult of the worst sort but also as one potentially loaded with racist overtones.

On the same theme, but on a lighter note, a training colleague once told me about a seminar he was running to prepare young businesspeople to live and work in Japan. At the coffee break one of the training team, a Japanese woman, overhead one of the participants reply to a comment on the chilly weather, "Yes, there is a nip in the air." When the seminar reconvened it was the Japanese trainer's turn to speak. She started her session with this statement, delivered with a wry smile, impeccable timing, and a measure of dryness: "Always remember that when you are in Japan and you say there is a 'nip' in the air, that there are 125 million of us on the ground!"

Our Self-Generating Beliefs

In addition to unfounded stereotypical beliefs that we acquire as children or as adults, we can also generate our own beliefs, sometimes very quickly, about almost anything. For example, a young female scientist told me of her experience working in a laboratory in Japan. She said that right from the beginning of her posting, she had noticed that her Japanese colleague, who was male, seemed reluctant to enter into conversation with her. At first she wondered if he was reluctant to speak to her simply because she was European (Italian) and not Japanese. She later revised this assessment and put it down to the fact that she was a woman in a male-dominated culture, and a blonde woman at that! This latter view seemed to be confirmed as she began to notice more the role that women played in Japanese society and how it was clearly different from that of the men. It was her growing belief that her Japanese colleague was sexist and probably racist too, and that deterred her from even attempting to break down the communication barrier between them. Each new day seemed to bring some new evidence, some small clue to confirm her belief that she was right in her assessment of the situation; the way he quickly looked away if she turned round in his direction; his silent uncommunicative presence when they were in the office alone; the way he and his other male colleagues engaged in long, easygoing discussions in Japanese too fast for her to follow, punctuated with laughter that always seemed to dry up when she turned to see what was going on. This always made her wonder, Are they are laughing at me? Maybe she thought her colleague was typical of all Japanese men.

In her second year there, quite by chance, they were finally thrown into a situation that gave them the opportunity to really talk to each other on a personal level. What she discovered came as a complete surprise. His initial reserve, he told her, had arisen out of basic shyness and a lack of confidence in his own social skills and foreign language ability. How could he be able to communicate with such a talented and confident European? What, he asked himself, should he say or not say, and how should he begin? As time passed, he felt he had delayed too long and had missed the moment. He had read her change in attitude toward him as one of disappointment and contempt. How could they both have been so wrong?

The Ladder of Inference

The Ladder of Inference is a useful model for understanding the stages that can lead to the generation of such beliefs. In *The Fifth Discipline Fieldbook* (1994), Peter Senge refers to the Ladder of Inference, which was first developed by Chris Argyris (1990). The Ladder of Inference describes a common mental pathway wherein a person selects some aspect or "data" from some behavior he has observed. He then adds meanings to the selected data and makes assumptions based on those meanings. He draws conclusions that lead him to adopt new beliefs about the world. Once he has adopted these beliefs, he begins to select only the data that reflect and support them. Finally, the person takes action based on the beliefs he has adopted. In practice the stages, or rungs of the ladder, are met in the following order:

1. You observe some behavior.
2. You focus on and select some aspects, or data, from the behavior you have observed.
3. You attach meaning or meanings to the aspects of the behavior you have selected which in turn are driven or influenced by your own cultural and personal perspectives and experience.
4. You then make assumptions based on the meanings you have ascribed.
5. You draw conclusions about the behavior based on the assumptions and meanings you have ascribed.
6. Your conclusions lead you to adopt new beliefs that you can apply generally in the world; in addition, these new beliefs will determine your focus and what aspects of behavior you choose to observe in the future.
7. Any further action you take is now based on the new beliefs you have generated and adopted.

Sometimes all it takes to start you off climbing the Ladder of Inference is a certain look or gesture from someone. For instance, at one of the first training programs I ever ran there was a participant who kept sighing loudly, and continued to do so throughout the day. After only the first sigh, however, I had started to race up the rungs of the Ladder of Inference:

- He was not a very nice person.
- He was very insensitive.
- He would spread bad publicity about me around the organization.

- He was trying to sabotage my course.
- He had taken a personal dislike to me.
- The content of my program was irrelevant to him.
- He had no respect for me.
- I was boring him.
- He was bored.

I never did find out why he kept sighing because I never got around to asking him. On reflection later, and because his course evaluation form was surprisingly positive, I realized that whatever his behavior meant, the knowledge could not have made me any more uncomfortable than I already was. And knowing what his sighing meant would have given me the information to evaluate my own behavior even if I ended up ignoring his sighs. And maybe his behavior had nothing to do with me or the course at all!

On another occasion I was traveling in India, and my travel budget had run rather low. I had passed a hot, tiring, but interesting day walking through the busy city of Bombay. I was amazed at the concentrated volume of traffic and had found myself, quite naturally, targeted by local salesmen operating on the street who thought I might, or indeed should, be interested in some local curios to take home as souvenirs. I was worried about my funds, so I contented myself with buying some oranges. As I walked back through the crowded streets I felt a tug at the back of my shirt. It did not take me long to scramble up the Ladder of Inference. Without even looking back to check, I had decided my thoughts supplied all I needed to know.

- Someone behind me is intent on selling me something I do not want.
- Everybody in this town sees me as a walking business opportunity.
- Why won't they leave me alone?
- They always pick on me.
- Here's another salesman.

At this stage I was still continuing to walk imperiously onward without looking back, but the tugging on my shirt became even more insistent. Eventually I stopped, fearing the shirt would be ripped from my back. Much to my amazement, it was not a salesman who confronted me but an old man in rags; from his condition I guessed he lived on the street. He held up an orange to me. For a few seconds I could not make sense of what my eyes were telling me; it did not relate to what I had already decided that I would—should—see. He pushed the orange toward me again, and then

I realized that the bag I had been carrying had burst; he had picked up the fallen orange and returned it to me. Humbled and a little ashamed, I offered him one of the other oranges from the bag, but with simple dignity he refused my offer—and turned and walked away.

Everybody has at some time jumped to the wrong conclusion about something and then acted on that wrong assumption. Think back and try to identify an occasion when you climbed the Ladder of Inference yourself and identify how each stage fed on the preceding one. Then also note how each progressive step carried you further away from the reality of the situation.

Tracking Your Progress Up the Ladder of Inference

Cross-cultural situations can provide us with almost limitless opportunities to start climbing the Ladder of Inference. Most travelers have had these thoughts:

> Why are they staring at me like that?
> If only I could understand the language. I know they are talking about me.
> I can see they don't like me because I'm a foreigner.

We are not machines. We cannot live without adding meaning or without drawing conclusions, nor should we try to; however, racing up the Ladder of Inference will not help us understand our culturally different co-workers or hosts when we are abroad—or help them understand us. Following are suggestions to help you check your reasoning as you move up the ladder.

Try to get into the habit of consciously noticing when you are making assumptions, adding your own meanings, and jumping to conclusions purely on the basis of subjective evidence. Ask yourself the following questions: Are my thoughts rational? Are they logical? Would a scientist agree with my logic? Easier said than done perhaps, but the more you try, the easier such self-questioning becomes. Reflecting on your own thinking and becoming aware of your reasoning is something that comes more naturally to some than to others. If you make a point of reflecting often during your cross-cultural interactions, then eventually the process will become habitual.

If others are giving you signals that cause you to start climbing the Ladder of Inference, consider what signals you are sending off. Perhaps your behavior is causing them to climb their own ladders. In other words, are you congruent in your communication? If not, then maybe the unexpected behavior you are seeing is simply the response that your own behavior has elicited.

Our signals can even be misinterpreted within our own cultural groups. Recently a person who knows me quite well said something like this: "I saw you were upset earlier, so I did not want to disturb you. Is everything all right now?" I must have looked at her in amazement. In fact, I had been doing a crossword puzzle and had not been upset at all. The nonverbal messages I had sent out, or the way they had been interpreted, had obviously indicated the opposite.

If appropriate, let your thinking, reasoning, and feelings be known to others so that they cannot be misinterpreted. This is clearly a high-risk strategy that in the wrong circumstances would only complicate matters. You first must judge the situation and the depth of the relationship you have with the others involved. In the culture in which you are communicating, have you ever seen anyone else successfully indulge in self-revelation? Would it be seen as acceptable behavior, or would it be viewed as unprofessional or overemotional? People in some cultures find it difficult to respond to a direct question, especially if they feel their answer may offend you. In such instances it may be more appropriate to take the indirect route by referring to a third party; for example, "What would Tanaka-san normally do in that situation?"

If you decide to use this approach, make sure you phrase the question as an interested inquiry rather than an accusation. The type of language you use will determine what emotional buttons you will press. For example, saying "You look annoyed" does not give the listener any information to explain why the speaker has come to such a conclusion. The statement expresses the speaker's evaluations, understandings, and perceptions about some unspecified behavior. Now compare it with the sentence, "I notice that you have turned away from me and no longer make eye contact." This *sensory-based language* provides descriptive rather than evaluative information. Notice it does not give the speaker's interpretation of what those action words mean. Shifting away from judgments and toward sensory-based descriptive language will enable you to communicate in a way that most people will experience as less offensive. A useful model for analyzing potentially uncomfortable cross-cultural situations is the D-I-E—Describe-Interpret-Evaluate—model. The steps are as follows:

Describe: What really happened? What did you actually *see*? Stick to the objective facts and resist adding anything else.

Interpret: Now decide what you *think* about what has happened; in other words, your interpretation of the events as you perceive them. This will naturally include your own cultural interpretation of the meaning of the event.

Evaluate: How do you *feel* about what has happened, and what makes you feel that way?

Finally, compare the three stages. Notice how different the description is from your interpretation and evaluation. All three stages will of course be influenced by your own values and standards, but this model will help you realize the level of influence. Also, using this model will help you avoid hasty judgments based on limited evidence and an immediate and personal reaction to an event.

Follow up with careful inquiries into other people's thoughts on the behavior that you have interpreted and drawn conclusions on. If possible, seek the advice and opinion of people from within the culture. Do they read the situation differently from you? What can you learn from the experience? If you employ an interpreter, or are with someone local who is acting as an informal interpreter, always ask for her reading of the behavior and mood of the other party and her impression of your performance, as well as a translation of the words spoken. Remember, any individual's perceptions are not necessarily right either.

Straitjacket Thinking

Straitjacket thinking is the way a person defines the boundary of his model of the world. The boundaries are often self-imposed and identify the person's comfort zone. To go beyond the boundary is to invite risk and maybe some dire consequence.

Car manufacturer Henry Ford reportedly once said, "If you think you can do it, or if you think you can't do it, then you're right." What he was saying was that people often set expectations for themselves that are less than they are capable of achieving; what people believe about themselves either propels them forward or holds them back. The traveler is by definition a cultural boundary crosser, and the way in which an individual thinks will define the number of choices she perceives for dealing with the challenges that arise. Study these examples of straitjacket thinking:

I can't eat that!

There's no way I'll stay there.

I must get back no later than 6 P.M.

I have to stay.

If something can go wrong, then it definitely will.

Those border officials always single me out.

I just know I'm not going to like it.

Well, it's either this or that, make up your mind.

We have all heard statements like these at one time or another, and probably most of us have used them ourselves. Often such statements represent nothing more than a safety valve, letting off steam, even a form of gallows humor. However, they can also be an outward indication that the speaker is limiting his options, and mentally walling himself in.

Cross-cultural interactions can be tiring and stressful, travel situations ambiguous, new environments unfamiliar, and others' behavior unexpected. To someone who habitually expects the worse to happen and is comfortable only with certainty and predictability, cross-cultural interactions can be very uncomfortable indeed. I am not going to suggest that people who have always tended to see the glass as half empty rather than half full, or seen things in terms of "either-or," should suddenly change the habit of a lifetime. However, on a practical level, we have already seen how our attitude can influence our behavior, which in turn can affect the attitude of the person at the receiving end of the behavior and subsequently their behavior back toward us. So if you are a pessimistic person and usually go to meet people for the first time with the expectation that you will not like them, things are likely to go less smoothly than they would if you went with an attitude of looking forward to meeting them.

Challenging Straitjacket Thinking

Although some researchers have suggested that the pessimists among us may actually perceive the world in more realistic terms, there are certainly times when it is helpful to bring to the surface and challenge the validity of self-imposed limits. If the limit is shown to be unreasonable then there is an opportunity to remove the block, or at least to move and stretch the boundary out farther. The best way of challenging this straitjacket thinking is by asking the right questions. First, however, you need to know how to spot and identify when straitjacket thinking is in operation. Let's assume that you are working on your own thinking patterns. Looking back, would you say that you tend to think using a lot of words like *must, should, necessary, impossible, can't,* and *won't*? Ask friends if they think that such words form a significant part of your vocabulary. It is these and similar "rule" words that tend to build limiting beliefs.

In the same way, reflect on your use of words like *every, always, all, never, each, none,* and *nowhere.* How much of your thinking do these words shape? Again, ask a friend. It is words like these that tend to limit thinking about new possibilities, a serious disadvantage to someone about to cross cultural frontiers. They limit because they give the impression that everything has been scoped and that there is nothing beyond the boundaries they describe.

Let us first challenge the rule words (*must, necessary, should, can't, won't,* etc.). For example, consider these statements: "I can't wait any longer" or "I have to stay." First, challenge the rule itself by asking, What stops me from waiting longer? What stops me from going?

Instead (or in addition) you could ask, What would happen if I did wait longer? What would happen if I went? These second questions challenge you to step beyond the rule and effectively outside the limits of your current boundaries. Practice adapting these two questions and applying them to some of your own statements that contain rule-type words.

Now let us challenge the next group of words (*all, always, every, none, never, each,* etc.) These superlative words tend to distort and limit our view of the world. Consider this statement: "Those border officials always single me out." In order to challenge the generalizing word *always*, ask, Was there ever a time when I was not singled out? Or you could simply repeat the word itself with an interrogative emphasis: Always? Once again, play around with versions of these questions to challenge some of your own statements that contain such superlatives.

Chapter 2 highlighted how you can be your own worst enemy in cross-cultural encounters. It could be the attitude you show to the locals, or it may be the way you, as a guest, are seen to behave, or even a combination of both that causes the hosts to distance themselves from you. Chapter 2 also looked at other self-imposed barriers such as those caused by the stereotypes and beliefs you carry and that influence your responses in cross-cultural interactions. Some of these beliefs are acquired through your upbringing, but others can be generated by the inferences you make based on your emotional reading of the circumstances you are in without any rational interpretation.

Sometimes the barriers are not visible to others at all but exist in your mind, instructing you as to what is and is not possible. These barriers limit your thinking and thus needlessly limit your possible options. However, with motivation and some effort, these self-imposed barriers can be reduced or removed.

Chapter 3 will explore positive traits that work to make you more effective in cross-cultural interactions.

CHAPTER
THREE

Important Cross-Cultural Traits

Successful culture crossers who are able to build strong intercultural relationships tend to share the following traits: they are open-minded and accepting of things or behavior that falls outside of familiar patterns or categories, they are able to be tolerant and remain calm in ambiguous situations, they are able to empathize with others, they can adapt their own behavior to suit different contexts and situations, they are aware of and perceptive regarding what is going on around them, and they take time to reflect on their experiences and learn from them.

Wide Categorization

In the previous discussions of stereotypes, I noted that people group the millions of stimuli to which they are exposed into categories in order to make sense of their world. However, some people have wider categories than others. A survival expert will have a far broader category of what may be considered potential food than the majority of people. In a cross-cultural context, the width of one's categorizations can be crucial. Narrow categorizers seeing unusual behavior in another culture are more likely to give meaning to that behavior according to their own cultural values and to be less open to the idea that the behavior or situation might have different meanings from those they have assigned. Their assessment of what is "normal" or allowable falls within narrow margins, thus making them more prone to in appropriate expectations and negative judgments. On the other hand, people whose categorizations are broad are more accepting of differences and of the idea that cross-cultural situations may have meanings that are completely different from their own.

Richard Detweiler (1980), in a study of U.S. Peace Corps volunteers on a remote island in the Pacific, found that those who were comfortable with broad categories were less likely to terminate their posting prematurely. They accepted the everyday differences more easily than those who categorized more narrowly. In addition, Ruben and Kealey (1979) found there was a positive correlation between this trait and task effectiveness in technical assistance advisers.

I was once running a cross-cultural awareness course in a rural part of Britain. In tune with the theme of the course, which focused on Japanese culture, and with the intention of fostering an international atmosphere over the lunch break, the organizers had provided what they described as a "Japanese-style buffet." The food had in fact been prepared by local caterers using local produce, most of it, as far as I could see, cooked in the local way as well. Nevertheless, they had gone to some effort to arrange and display the buffet in a suitably "Oriental" way. Imagine my surprise and dismay when I overheard four of the participants say words to the effect, "I'm not eating that foreign stuff" and then openly pull a face and avoid the buffet. They ate instead from the bowls of chips and snack foods. They clearly had a narrow, self-imposed, and somewhat illogical opinion of what constitutes acceptable food. If they ever visited Japan, such behavior would not endear them to the Japanese. I suspect these people would probably find eating anywhere outside of Britain, let alone travel itself, an uncomfortable experience.

Having broad categories is conducive to tolerance in cross-cultural situations. People who have a tolerant personality have access to many more dimensions in thinking about an issue; they realize that the stereotypes they hold should be open to modification. They are comfortable in ambiguous situations, patient with others, and broad-minded when considering new concepts. The width of a person's categorizations will have a major impact on how well he interacts with people from other cultures.

Tolerance of Ambiguity

Connected to the ability to set broad categories is tolerance for ambiguity, which simply means being comfortable with and able to handle situations where you are not in possession of all the facts and have no idea what the big picture is or what will happen next.

Most people in ambiguous situations experience some level of discomfort; however, those with a low tolerance for ambiguity will experience higher levels of discomfiture and probably be less able to adapt to new situations. On the other hand, people with a high tolerance for ambiguity will find such situations less stressful; the added stimulation may actually be attractive. Tolerance of ambiguity is all about the ability to cope in unpredictable, unstructured, and uncertain situations. Cross-cultural interactions are loaded with uncertainty and ambiguities—a potential nightmare for those who need a high level of control, certainty, and structure in their lives and in their interactions.

I remember an occasion when a local office was expecting a visit from a senior executive from overseas. Determined to give the executive VIP treatment, the staff designed a schedule for his visit and faxed it to him for comment. He replied with his approval almost immediately. The preparations began in earnest. The office staff planned to exceed the visitor's expectations so that when he left, he would have a favorable impression of the office, its staff, and the country. The high point of the visit was to be a dinner, specially arranged off site with no expense spared, where the visitor would meet some local celebrities. The visit went smoothly right up to the point when the office manager suggested that it was time to proceed to the restaurant for the meal. The executive looked both surprised and uncomfortable, "I saw dinner on the schedule but I did not realize it was to be off site." This was true; although the office manager had included the dinner in the schedule, he had deliberately not given any details, preferring to reveal his plan at the appropriate moment as a sort of surprise treat. Unfortunately, the slight air of mystery seemed to stress the executive, who proceeded to fire a barrage of questions at the manager: "Where is it being held? Is it in a safe area? How long will it take to travel to this place and back? Who else will be there? What are their roles? What is their connection to this office? What sort of food does this establishment serve?" Only after the manager had responded to these and other questions to the executive's satisfaction did the executive allow himself to be driven to the venue. When the visitor eventually returned home, the office manager called his staff together in a meeting to discuss how the visit had gone. The general consensus was that everything had gone well up to the mention of the meal arrangements, and from then on things had taken a turn for the worse. The group's opinion of the executive himself was not discussed, but I suspect their opinion of him also changed when the meal arrangements were mentioned.

Empathy

Empathy is the term used to describe the ability to be able to view a situation or problem from another's point of view. In cross-cultural interactions, this means being able to imagine or experience something from another's frame of reference or worldview.

Empathy is not to be confused with sympathy, although the difference between the two may appear to be subtle. In showing sympathy, you attempt to understand another by imagining how you would feel if you were in the other person's position. If this person is from your own culture and hometown and is someone with whom you have a lot in common, then what you feel may in fact be a close approximation to what the other actually is feeling. However, when communicating with someone from another culture, sympathy, which is based on an assumption of similarity, is an ethnocentric approach. It is ethnocentric because you have not changed your cultural frame of reference but have simply assumed others' will be similar to your own. Another important difference is the purpose that drives the two. The purpose of sympathy is to find common ground, shared experiences, and a form of agreement. The purpose of empathy, on the other hand, is not about agreeing with people; it is about trying to fully understand someone else's perspective, both emotionally and intellectually.

Earlier in the book I listed empathy as a skill, a behavior, an attitude, and a trait. Because it can be developed as a skill, empathy requires a high level of sensitivity to nonverbal behavior. It also requires an attitude of respect for self and others and an open mind. I listed it as a trait because it is clear that some people are able to empathize well while others are not. Daniel Goleman (1996) suggests that empathy as a trait is developed in young children from around the age of two and a half years. It is often the result of how a child is raised. Children whose parents pointed out, while disciplining them, the distress their misbehavior had caused someone else tended to display more empathetic ability than those whose parents did not initiate such training. A child's ability to empathize is also shaped by seeing how others react in response to someone else's distress. Over time children develop their own repertoire of empathic responses.

I suspect that people in group-oriented cultures, where extended families are the norm, are in general more empathetic. It would make an interesting study to see if this is the case.

To check your own response, listen to yourself advising people. If your suggestion tends to be along the lines of "If I were in your position, I'd . . ." or "What I think you should do is this . . . ," then you are giving advice based on the assumption that their world is similar to your own. However, statements such as "I wonder what they really think about . . ." or "From your point of view it must appear completely different" are approaches that indicate you are adopting an empathetic approach and are trying to understand the reality inside someone else's head instead of merely projecting your own.

A key element of empathy is the ability to see things from different perspectives. If you want to develop your own empathetic ability, the key is to direct the focus of your attention away from yourself and toward the other person, and to listen without projecting your understanding of a situation onto the other person's description of it. Try this exercise to see yourself from another perspective. Remember back to a time when you had a disagreement or argument with a friend or work colleague. As you recall the situation, what you said, and how you felt when you said it, imagine that you have become the other person listening to you. It usually helps to physically move to where the other person was sitting relative to you and to adopt his posture and body language. Listen to yourself from the other person's perspective and see if it affects your previous perception of the dispute.

I tested this technique a few years ago in relation to a long and frustrating telephone sales conversation I had had the previous month and that had left me angry and annoyed at the caller's constant questions. First I played the scenario through from my perspective, which actually started to get me wound up all over again. I then got up and sat in a chair facing where I had just been and imagined listening to myself at the other end of the phone. I then imagined asking one of the questions I remember the other caller had asked. Again, from his perspective, I listened to my response. All of a sudden I realized in a flash of insight that he had no choice but to respond as he did because I, not wanting to be drawn into anything, was defensive, indirect, and evasive in my replies. The more I listened to myself, the more I started to appreciate how confusing my responses must have been; was I interested in the product or not? My indirectness had given him no clues at all, so he had little option but to keep asking me questions.

As I mentioned in Chapter 1, those people who are confident of their ability to empathize with others tend to be more relaxed and less defensive when meeting people for the first time. As a result, the meeting is easier and less stressful for the other person, too. To make others more comfortable around you should be the general aim of cross-cultural sojourners who are trying to understand and integrate into another culture.

Behavioral Flexibility

Psychologists hold a number of competing views as to what motivates behavior. At one end of the scale is the behaviorist view that behavior is just a series of observable reflex actions. At the other end of the scale is the view that that the mind has an effect on overt behavior. Since life is complicated enough, I will stick to definitions for the moment and simply define behavior as some form of observable action. According to current psychological theory, your behavior is influenced by a number of factors: your past experience, your response to those past experiences, and your current circumstances. Together these factors confirm and reinforce your usual patterns of behavior. Though you may have a natural tendency to behave in a particular way to certain situations, this does not mean that you have to respond in that way. Once you become consciously aware of your normal or natural behavior, you then have the opportunity to choose whether to retain the behavior or replace it with something more appropriate, especially if your usual behavior is not serving you well in specific situations.

Generally speaking, most people do not require radical change to their normal patterns of behavior in order to deal with day-to-day situations. Instead, they alter their behavioral response to suit the situation. For example, they may choose to be more social in some contexts than they are in others. They may choose to be more social to certain people than they are to others. This flexibility of behavior is normal and, in fact, indicates a high level of social skill. For those who want to integrate into another culture, it is essential not only that they have the ability to adapt their behavior but also that the parameters within which they can be flexible are wide rather than narrow.

Unfortunately, some people find it difficult to adjust their behavior in this way and so always respond in the same way regardless of whether the circumstances have changed or not. For example, they may be unsociable in most situations or overly sociable even when such behavior is inappropriate.

According to William Schutz (1966), our earliest experiences—in particular, what we learn from parents or guardians during our formative years—are critical in shaping what we come to feel about ourselves and, as a result, the patterns of behavior we tend to adopt. People who grow up with poor self-esteem and feel that people do not like them are likely to adopt some sort of defense mechanism. For example:

1. They take the position of the *victim*. If they feel themselves to be unlikable, then other people must not like them either; in other words, they have projected their poor concept of themselves onto the people they come into contact with.
2. They *displace* and *transfer* the poor concept they have of themselves onto others and then become critical of them: "I don't like you; you're not a nice person."
3. They assume that others feel as bad about themselves as they do and so feel that they can *identify* with them on that basis. Their perceived role thus becomes one of *helper:* "I know you do not like yourself, but I understand and I can help."

Adopting a defense mechanism usually results in rigid and inflexible behavior. A poor self-concept can affect a person's behavior in these three areas in the following ways:

1. If a person feels insignificant, she may not be able to adjust her level of sociability in different situations. She may become stuck being either not social enough or overly social.
2. If a person feels incompetent, she may be unable to shift her behavior between accepting direction from others and being more self-directed and able to direct others
3. If a person feels unlikable or unlovable, she may be unable to move between less open and more open behavior, depending on the situation and the other people involved. Her behavior may become stuck so that she is either impersonal or inappropriately overly personal most of the time.

Such behavior patterns are significant when crossing cultures. If a person has a poor self-concept in his own country, then it is unlikely to miraculously improve once he sets foot in another culture. I hinted at this in my description of the Concerned Missionary in my caricatures of traveler types in Chapter 2. In a new and more challenging environment, he may indeed find that his self-concept improves, but the change will not be instantaneous. A person can, however, suddenly change the way he behaves if he decides that his current behavior is not helpful. If this change produces positive

- **Arena**—what is known to self and to others
- **Blind spot**—what is unknown to self but apparent to others
- **Facade**—what is known to self but hidden to others ("under the table")
- **Unknown**—what is unknown to self and to others; potentially available but not yet discovered

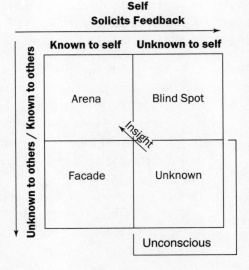

Figure 3-1   The Johari Window

results, then over time, it is likely to have a positive effect on his self-concept as well.

Unfortunately, it is difficult to know how flexible your own patterns of behavior are and how your behavior is experienced by others. Even if you ask, it is often difficult for people to provide feedback on sensitive issues like this. What you need to find out is how others perceive and experience your behavior and how their perception is different from your own. The Johari Window (Figure 3-1) is a model that helps explain this dilemma. Following are strategies for discovering what lies in the blind spot—in particular, how flexible and accommodating or how rigid and inflexible your behavior is as perceived by others.

1. Practice self-reflection, mentally monitor your own behavior in cross-cultural interactions, analyze yourself. For example, how would you characterize your relationships with others? Would you say that people are comfortable being around you? Do you tend to get involved in more arguments than your friends and colleagues? Do you maintain good working relationships with your work colleagues? In response to the answers these and other questions generate, follow up with this type of question: On what evidence have I based my

answers? Would this evidence stand the scrutiny of a courtroom lawyer's questioning?

2. Solicit feedback from a range of other people who have experience of your behavior.

3. Attend an interpersonal skills course that includes participation in role plays where you later receive feedback.

4. Take a psychometric test such as the Fundamental Interpersonal Relations Orientation-Behavior (FIRO-B). Contact addresses are at the back of this book.

Sensory Acuity

Sensory acuity is a skill that enables you to make finer and more useful distinctions in the information you receive via your senses. It is linked to many of the topics I will discuss in Chapter 4, in particular, existential alertness and the sensing function of the Myers-Briggs Type Indicator. It is also clearly linked to what could be described generically as listening skills. Those who are regarded as good communicators are able to adapt their message and delivery in midflow in response to the nonverbal signals they receive from their audience. When they ask questions, they do not just listen to the words in the reply, but they also look at the whole message that is being presented. They notice the supporting facial expressions, posture, and gestures that are used. They also notice the tonality of the response, the speed at which it was delivered, the volume and power of the voice, subtle intonations, and any hesitance. Most of us do this without realizing it, but sometimes we engage in other activities at the same time that distract our attention—for example, we're planning our next question or anticipating what the other person will say next and where her answer may eventually lead.

The intention that lies behind why you are paying such close attention to the other person is also important. There is a subtle, but noticeable, difference between being an audience to a highly skilled communicator— someone whose sole intention is to make a favorable impression or to manipulate—and conversing with someone who is genuinely interested in what you are saying and your views. The first can leave you with a vague, uneasy feeling that you have been "psychologically mugged"; the second approach will leave you with a positive impression of someone sincerely trying to build a bridge of understanding.

The straightforward approach to reading a person's nonverbal communication is to consciously notice all the aspects of the behavior shown and then to test your tentative conclusions by asking questions. At this stage it is not necessary for the other person to be from another culture; in fact, it's probably better to practice on a friend first.

Many people have a tendency to label nonverbal behavior far too quickly on the basis of one or two gestures: "She must be lying because she touched her nose" or "I can tell he is very confident by the way he steeples his fingers and leans back in his chair." Single gestures such as these, when taken in isolation, are not reliable indicators on which to base judgments. As you become more experienced, you can look for clusters of gestures and patterns of behavior. With experience, you are also less likely to fall into the trap of labeling too early.

In order to be aware of all the potentially visible nonverbal behavior being displayed, it is important to have a relaxed and open attitude. With this attitude, your peripheral vision can spot small movements around the person's whole body. If you are tense or concentrating too hard, there is a tendency to also narrow your focus so that you end up concentrating on one or two aspects only, and are likely to miss other clues. I cannot emphasize too strongly that to do this effectively, you must be relaxed and natural, not only to collect the information, but also to avoid making your subject uncomfortable. Anyone who has been at the receiving end of an intense, focused stare knows how disconcerting it can be. If you want to make friends and build cultural bridges, then you need to stay relaxed to pick up these clusters of minute movement in a natural, unaffected way.

So what sorts of clues, what patterns of behavior could you be looking for? You could, for example, notice changes in behavior, or differences from the overall behavior pattern, as well as what seems to excite the other person. Note changes in skin color or eye movements, in hand gestures, in breathing rate and depth. Where is the person's attention—on you, on somewhere else in the room, or seemingly focused on internal thoughts?

The purpose of heightening your sensory awareness in this way is to enable you to build rapport with others by adjusting your own behavior so you can remain in synchronization with them at a physical and mental level. I also believe that an awareness of where their attention is and how they respond to you during conversation will give you clues that will enable you to better empathize with your hosts and glimpse the world through their eyes.

The old Chinese proverb, "Two thirds of what we see is already behind our eyes," is wonderfully apt when applied to the traveler who has just landed in a new and strange country. Things appear strange only because they are different from what the traveler is used to seeing. If they were not different, then they would probably go unnoticed. When you arrive in a country for the first time, what you notice and focus on is a function of your own personality and cultural programming. In other words, what you notice probably says more about you than it does about the host culture. Often cultural differences are experienced on a subliminal as well as a conscious level. In fact, the first things that you will tend to notice are physical expressions of culture: clothing, architecture, advertisements, general noise level, music, climate, smells, and so forth.

Consciously using your senses to observe what is going on around you when you are abroad will not only add to your knowledge of the country and its culture, it will also intensify your enjoyment of the sojourn experience because you will start to notice detail in the sensory stimuli that you would previously have overlooked.

The Ability to Learn from Experience

I remember meeting a young traveler who was nearing the end of an around-the-world backpacking tour. I was also backpacking at the time, but I was close to the start of my trip. We had both arrived on the island of Tahiti in French Polynesia just before sunrise. There was a music festival over the weekend, which meant that it was very difficult to find any vacancies in budget accommodation of the sort that I could afford. It was very early in the morning when I started to walk up and down the small back streets of Papeete, the capital, but despite my long search I could find no vacancies. Eventually I sat down by the waterfront to work out my next move. That was when I met the other traveler. She was from Sweden and had arrived in Tahiti from Australia. Before that she had been in Indonesia, Singapore, and Thailand. Straightaway she told me that she was thinking of catching the next plane home, but then she started to tell me some of her travel experiences and adventures. She seemed to have difficulty in separating one experience from another. It was as if she had lost track of time and all the experiences had telescoped together. Was it in Thailand or Indonesia that she had lost her passport? She had met someone called John in Sydney—or was it Perth? The best beach she had ever seen was, was, now where was it? A bungee jump in . . . well, it was a famous gorge somewhere. Suddenly she turned to me and said, "I think I'll go to the airport and get the next plane home. I need time to think." She seemed very tired and so was I, but I was still surprised she wanted to leave right away. Neither of us had ever visited Tahiti before and she had literally just arrived. "But look around," I said, "the place looks beautiful. It's Tahiti and you may never get the chance to come here again." We discussed it a little further, but so much for my powers of persuasion; she went back to the airport and I never saw her again.

I thought about the incident, though, and I wondered if she was suffering from more than sheer exhaustion—experience fatigue perhaps. Ever since leaving her home in Sweden, her life had consisted of one new experience after another, a constant deluge of sensory stimulation, new places, new cultures, new friends, and always traveling, moving on. No wonder she was tired.

This experience, that life is like a roller coaster, is common to many travelers and businesspeople abroad for the short term. They have lots of new and stimulating experiences, but often never get—or take—the time to reflect on them. As a result, these experiences never become anything more than a series of mental snapshots and a growing stock of travel anecdotes of the sort the World-Weary Traveler and the Sardonic Old Hand would love to have. I have seen evidence of this myself when I have been in the audience of someone giving a talk about a country and culture where he has lived and worked for many years. In such talks it quickly becomes apparent whether or not the speaker has actually reflected on his experience and sought to find out the underlying reasons for any differences between the hosts' behavior and his own. These speakers provide more information that is of practical value to others going to live in the same country than those speakers who never reflected on their experiences or sought to uncover the "why" behind the behavior they saw. If you want to learn from your experiences as well as enjoy them, you need to take time to think through them. What happened? Why did it happen? What does it mean? What should I do if I am ever in the same situation again?

A good way of capturing the learning potential from your own experience is to keep a personal learning log. This could be in the form of a diary, but I suggest the format shown in Figure 3-2 to really maximize the potential of such a log.

The thinking behind this approach is based on the theory of how adults learn from their experiences. Most people probably regard the learning that

Date 2003	Activity undertaken (What happened?)	What I learned (What does it mean?)	How and when can I apply this knowledge?
16 June	Failed in my 2nd attempt to arrange an initial meeting with Mr. Suzuki, a manager in another organization. Asked colleague Mr. Tanaka for advice.	Tanaka-san felt that perhaps a less direct approach would be more effective. He advised me to find someone known and respected by Mr. Suzuki to arrange an appointment for me.	In order to expand my network of contacts, I may need to use a third party to act as a referee and broker for me.
17 June	Attended a meeting arranged by Sato-san. During introductions I was surprised by the behavior of Mr. Sugano, who . . .		

Figure 3-2   Personal Learning Log

they get from their experiences as something that occurs automatically, albeit accidentally, in the normal course of living, and of course this is partially true. In particular, unpleasant experiences usually prompt us to alter or modify our behavior so we don't repeat the same experience. For example, you visit a restaurant for the first time and find that the service is poor and the food badly cooked, and within hours you are suffering from food poisoning. The chances are you will never visit that restaurant again; once was enough, and you've learned from the experience.

Kolb (1984) illustrates this in his model of the learning cycle (Figure 3-3). However, if all your learning were like this, you would always be learning retrospectively. Do you really want to be reactive rather than prepared; always learning to cope, rather than developing and growing?

Learning as you go, without being conscious of the fact, is fine, but just imagine if you were to start consciously connecting and integrating the two processes—doing and learning. You would become, in effect, a "learning opportunist." In a cross-cultural context, this connection is of enormous value. It adds an interesting, enlightening dimension to all those experiences that expatriates have—experiences that may otherwise remain as merely

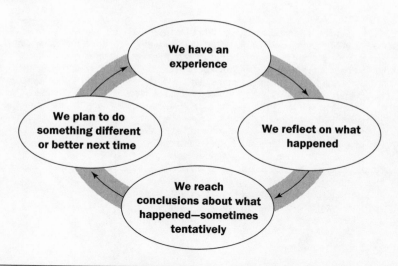

Figure 3-3   How We Learn from Experience

interesting anecdotes, providing entertainment but lacking any follow-up application.

When you become a learning opportunist, learning becomes a more deliberate process. You purposefully start to extract learning from even unremarkable, routine events, and you learn from your successes as well as from your mistakes. It also means that you can articulate what you have learned, so that you can pass on your experience in a useful format to counterparts and successors or even to family and friends who come to visit you. Most people, after a couple of years in a different culture, forget what it was that they found strange and difficult to cope with when they first arrived, because what was strange becomes normal and no longer merits their attention.

Figure 3-4 shows how this learning develops through four stages. Stage 1: On arrival in a new country you have yet to discover what you need to know about the culture to be able to function effectively. You have no idea of the thinking behind the culturally driven behavior that you see. You may even continue to behave exactly as you would back home, despite the fact that your behavior now elicits a different reaction from what you would normally expect. Stage 2: You start to become aware of the gaps in your knowledge of the culture and social conventions of the host nationals. It is now clear to you that some social skills you took for granted back home no

1—Denial	4—Commitment / Contentment
Unconscious incompetence	Unconscious competence
"No, this doesn't make sense."	"But of course . . . it's natural."

2—Resistance / Discomfort	3—Acceptance / Exploration / Delight
Conscious incompetence	Conscious competence
"Well, maybe, but . . ."	"This does make sense now."

Figure 3-4   Assimilating New Learning

longer work in your new home, and you find this frustrating. Stage 3: As your knowledge and understanding increase, you begin to acquire new social skills and to feel that you are making progress and getting things done. Stage 4: Although you are still continuing to learn new things about the culture, you now tend to respond automatically in a way that is acceptable to the host nationals in most day-to-day situations. You no longer feel any stress about what you still do not know, because continuing to learn is, in itself, a source of satisfaction.

As your learning follows the curve from left to right, it passes through four stages until the new learning is absorbed into your normal behavior and becomes automatic. As a consequence, the advice you may now pass on to others may omit useful information. The problem lies in the fact that once you have solved the initial problems of settling in, the solutions become part of your daily life. If you had kept a learning log and referred back to it, it would have reminded you of those problems and the process by which you solved them.

Referring back to Kolb's learning cycle, consider if, instead of simply reflecting on and reaching conclusions on each new experience, you thought ahead to see how what you have learned could best be applied in a similar situation. This is a more proactive approach to learning from your own experience. You would, in effect, be coaching yourself around the cycle, as shown in Figure 3-5.

This revised learning cycle fits in neatly with the format of the personal learning log outlined earlier in this chapter.

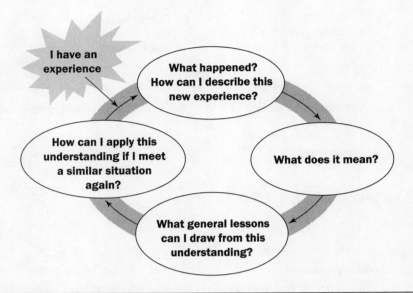

Figure 3-5   Coaching Yourself through the Cycle

Managing from the Inside

You may be thinking that categorizing within narrow parameters and having a high tolerance for ambiguity and empathy are all inherent personality traits about which a person can do little. It's true that these traits are part of some people's personality. However, I disagree with the view that you cannot do anything to enhance your effectiveness. The first step is to become aware of your own tendencies and characteristics, accept that they are an integral part of your personality and appreciate them as such.

The second step is to reflect on your own reactions in past cross-cultural situations when you were confronted with new or inexplicable behaviors, events, or conditions. What conclusions or judgments, if any, did you make, and how comfortable were you in those situations? If still possible, you could request feedback from others. Also, you may wish to complete a psychometric questionnaire—a sort of personal inventory—to obtain a structured breakdown of your personality type. Bear in mind that many psychometric instruments give only a glimpse of one aspect of your personality rather than the "whole you"; other influences such as your cultural background, upbringing, religion, education, and life experiences may not be picked up by the instrument. However, the results may still be valuable in helping you to better understand yourself in a more structured way.

The Myers-Briggs Type Indicator

One of the most widely used personal development psychometrics in the world is the Myers-Briggs Type Indicator (MBTI). I believe that it is very useful in helping people to understand their own and others' tendencies and characteristics. It may predict how they will respond to stress and to challenges common in cross-cultural encounters, such as handling situations that are unstructured or that test their flexibility. I will describe the Myers-Briggs Type Indicator in considerable detail for a number of reasons. First, I want to give a flavor of the type of information it can provide. Second, it is a well-researched and respected instrument that has withstood the test of time. Third, I will be referring to the dimensions in different contexts later in the book.

The original goal behind the MBTI was to help people to understand typical patterns of human difference and to value their own gifts as well as the different gifts of others. Psychological type suggests that we all have a pattern by which we connect with, perceive, and act on the world. The MBTI attempts to identify that pattern by establishing which poles of the following four dimensions we are attracted to first, or feel most comfortable with. It is accepted that everyone shifts between the two poles of all four dimensions throughout the day; however, each of us is born with a preference for one of the poles over its opposite.

E	**Extraversion**	*Direction of energy flow*	**Introversion**	I
S	**Sensing**	*How we take in information*	**Intuition**	N
T	**Thinking**	*How we make decisions*	**Feeling**	F
J	**Judging**	*Orientation to the outside world*	**Perceiving**	P

Extraversion Versus Introversion

These habits of mind, sometimes referred to as our orientation of energy, are not a measure of gregarious or shy behavior, but have more to do with how we charge our mental batteries. Extraverts seek stimulation and energy outside of themselves and so have a greater motivation to initiate contact with others. They are usually the ones who arrange parties and get-togethers because they feel more motivation to do so than introverts. As a result, they can appear more proactive than the more reflective introverts. In meetings and in general discussion, whether at home or abroad, the way in which extraverts contribute can be a clue as to their preference for Extraversion. They tend to interrupt more often and construct sentences as they speak, sometimes with the result that they immediately wish that they had not said what they did. On the other hand, those who are drawn more toward Introversion are stimulated and recharge their batteries from within. They are more inclined to receive and reflect. In group discussions they may find it difficult to get a word in over their extraverted friends and colleagues. When they do speak, their sentences are usually well constructed and thought out—that is, introverts tend to mentally check what they are going to say before they actually say it.

I once had a conversation with a Greek national, Konstantine, who had been living in the United Kingdom for nearly ten years. He told me that when he wanted to think about a problem or question at work, sometimes he would lean back in his chair, put his hands behind his head, and close his eyes. In his early days at work in the United Kingdom, his reverie was always interrupted by one of his British colleagues exclaiming, "Hey Konstantine, don't fall asleep on the job" or "Get working! The boss might come." He knew their comments were meant to be humorous, but the fact that they had bothered to say them at all made him suspect they contained an undercurrent of seriousness. His stock response was, "I'm thinking," but his colleagues advised, "You can't just sit there doing nothing, you have to at least look busy." Ruefully he asked me, "Which is best, first I think and then I do something, or I do something first and then I think about it?" He soon realized that in a busy office, just sitting and doing some quiet, introverted thinking can be interpreted by others as doing nothing productive at all.

Cross-cultural effectiveness requires a desire or motivation to make contact and connect at a personal level (Extraversion). It also requires the ability and willingness to reflect and make sense of what is happening externally (Introversion)—for example, pausing to determine your most effective response to an unexpected or unfamiliar situation as opposed to just giving in to a knee-jerk reaction. Knowing to which of these poles you are most drawn will enable you not only to play to your strengths, but also to be more aware of, and attend to, those areas you may be tempted to neglect. For example, extraverts may need to use more effort to refrain from blurting out whatever comes to mind. Spontaneity is not valued to the same extent in every culture. In some cultures, a careless comment can result in a loss of face for those you are communicating with. Remember, concern for your impact on others should always be a high priority if you want to build cross-cultural relationships.

Although I personally have a preference toward Introversion, when I arrive in a country for the first time, I find my attention is more in the outside world as I try to make contact, communicate, and reorient myself. Every sojourner quickly needs answers to similar questions on entering a new culture for the first time: What is the true value of the local money?

Where will I sleep? What can I eat? Will I be able to communicate and make myself understood by the host nationals? How can I get from A to B? It is usually only after answers to these questions have been obtained that the sojourner's attention turns to the deeper questions of values. Why do the local people behave and react the way that they do? Do people here trust me yet? What is the best place to meet and make new friends? Who can I ask about the correct protocol for bringing up a sensitive topic for discussion? These are the types of questions that tend to surface later and from which cultural learning can grow. These deeper questions require that the traveler reflect on what he has seen and experienced so that he can assign meaning and make sense of it (Introversion). The practical issues that hit the traveler on arrival, however, are not solved by quiet internal reflection, but by connecting with the outside world and communicating externally (Extraversion).

Sensing Versus Intuition

This dimension and the next one (Thinking/Feeling) are usually referred to as *mental functions*. According to Jungian theory, on which the Myers-Briggs Type Indicator is based, we use our minds in two basic ways: We take in information and then we come to some conclusion or decision about that information.

We also take in information in two basic ways. The first way is perhaps the most obvious one: We take in information through our senses of sight, hearing, touch, taste, and smell. For example, if you hear someone say, "I won't believe it until I see it with my own eyes" or "Let me test it first," they mean that they will only be happy with evidence or information that they can take in and verify with their own senses. Those who prefer information that comes via their senses tend to be the practical, hands-on type. In company training workshops on, say, change management, they are usually the ones who ask questions like, "You haven't told us what was wrong with the way we were doing things before; if it's not broken, then why fix it?" and "Have we got the resources to implement this new process properly?"

The second way of taking in information is through our subconscious, using our intuition. For example, we may form an impression about another person minutes or even seconds after meeting them. If asked by a third person to explain the evidence for our impression, we would probably be hard-pressed to supply any solid or tangible data to support our view. Subconsciously we may have seen some pattern of behavior in the way the stranger is relating to us that we have encountered at some time in our past.

Our intuition picks up meanings, relationships, and possibilities that go beyond the sensory information. In a world where it is becoming increasingly easy to obtain vast amounts of information quickly, certain professions such as business intelligence, financial planning, and criminal detective work (to name but three) have realized that what they need is not so much the people who can gather more information, but those who can do something with it—for example, those who naturally see the patterns and correlations in data. These are usually people with a preference for taking in information via intuition. They are future oriented because they are always looking to connect the next dot in order to complete the bigger picture. At company training workshops on change management, they tend to ask questions like these: What can we use it for? Are there any other possibilities we haven't thought about? How can you be so certain about the future? Things might change.

A close friend of mine accepted some part-time work that she could do from home. The work consisted of assembling electrical circuit boards by hand. Each board required that the various components first be placed on a board in a precise order followed by a lot of precision soldering. Although there was a variety of boards, she tended to concentrate on one type of board at a time so that she could build up speed. Often when I visited she would have the blank boards laid out on the table and a smoking soldering iron in her hand, so I always offered to help out. Invariably, within five or ten minutes I was totally bored, my intuitive preference impatient to do something else. At this point she would usually spot some minute but critical omission on one of the boards I had just completed. I once asked her why the work didn't drive her crazy with boredom. She replied that she actually found making the circuit boards engrossing, relaxing, and a good way of reducing stress—a response from someone with a clear preference for Sensing.

So, in summary, we have those who prefer taking in information through their senses and those who prefer to rely on their intuition. Sensing types tend to live more in the here and now and are often seen as realistic and practical. They are good at working with facts and are careful with detail, preferring to use tried and true, established procedures rather than novel approaches. They need to be convinced that change is a practical solution before they wholeheartedly go along with it. Intuitive types, on the other hand, value novelty and change. They like to see the big picture and to grasp the overall patterns. Through the use of their intuition they become adept at seeing new possibilities and are often future oriented.

For cross-cultural effectiveness, both Sensing and Intuition are needed. All of us, despite our dominant preference, have access to both poles of this dimension. For example, most education systems will challenge us to gather specific facts and details (Sensing) and to understand conceptual frameworks and models (Intuition), which we then apply (Sensing). Then we may generate other possible uses for the model (Intuition). When we are abroad, we need our sensory acuity to notice our own state and the states of others. To be able to empathize with people, we need sensory awareness and the ability to consciously modify our behavior if necessary (Sensing). We also need to be able to gauge mood and atmosphere and pick up on patterns of behavior and responses (Intuition).

Of course, there are limitless other instances where we need to access either preference. I have noticed that even though I normally have a stronger preference for using my intuition, when I first land in a strange country my Sensing function comes to the fore. I find that in this state of heightened awareness, my ability to take in information and remember detail is greatly enhanced. In fact, this is one of the aspects of traveling that I enjoy most—living in the moment and fully experiencing the present. As a natural intuitive, I am normally not very detail conscious, as anyone who knows me well will verify. However, after only a short period in a new country I am often amazed to find that I can remember and recite a mass of facts and details about my new environment that I could not have learned so thoroughly in an academic context. Later, after the initial impact of arrival has worn off and I have time to reflect, my usual preference of Intuition moves to the fore. Usually this preference seems to work quietly, without prompting, in the back of my mind. I may be eating, showering, or resting when I suddenly realize that I have seen a pattern of behavior repeated by several of the host nationals. I then try to link it to what was going on at the time in each case. Usually I make a mental a note to follow up by asking a local if I am right and by making more observations to check if the behavior is consistent in different contexts.

Thinking Versus Feeling

Having acquired information through either Sensing or Intuition, we then have to do something with it, maybe decide on the quality of the information itself or make some decision based on it. This dimension, then, is really about how we prefer to make decisions. One way of making decisions is on the basis of cause and effect, by carefully weighing the evidence, all the pros and cons, and any people issues to be solved. People who use this approach are referred to as the Thinking type and tend to focus on the logical consequences of any choice or action. They seek an objective standard of truth and are good at analyzing what is wrong with something. They respect rules and will work to change those rules they disagree with.

A good manager who has a preference for Thinking will value justice, integrity, and fairness; has a natural ability to adopt a "third-person" position and will handle people issues with impartiality; and, when necessary, can take a long-term view of a situation.

Another way of making decisions is to base your decision on what you feel about the issue in question. This is an equally rational approach, because why make a decision that's going to make you feel bad? The difference is that it is based on person-centered values and not on logical objectivity. People who use this approach are referred to as the Feeling type; they tend to consider how important the choices are to themselves and others. They like dealing with people, are interested in understanding people, and are often naturally empathetic and sympathetic. Good managers who have a preference for Feeling will value harmony and tact and prefer diplomacy to confrontation. If the rules get in their way or prevent them from handling an issue appropriately, they simply ignore the rules or bend them to suit. The motivation that drives Feeling types to focus on the impact of their decisions on others also moves them to spontaneously appreciate what someone else has just said, even though they may then realize the statement did not make sense. I was using Myers-Briggs in a team-building course when, in the middle of writing some statistics on the board, a voice called out that my calculations were wrong. The caller was right of course, and I amended the figures accordingly. The incident, however, prompted a discussion among the group as to why none of them had spotted the error. They pointed out, with all due respect to the person who announced the mistake, that his ability at calculating was no better than theirs. In the end the difference seemed primarily a matter of where their attention had been focused. One other person did admit to noticing the error but hadn't wanted to embarrass me by pointing it out. The person who did was the only Thinking type in the room.

In terms of cross-cultural effectiveness, both aspects of this dimension have a role to play. The Thinking approach is useful in a situation where emotions are high or near the surface. The ability to sit back and remove yourself, at least emotionally, from the situation and weigh the issues involved both logically and objectively is usually far more influential and constructive than attempting to justify your or anyone else's subjective values. Subjective values are difficult to articulate and may not be shared by the other party.

The Feeling approach is the one that will help you to build rapport, empathize, and ultimately understand the other party. It also provides the interest and motivation to focus on people, personalities, and emotions rather than just the task at hand. Usually it is the important people issues that in the end make the difference between success and failure.

Judging Versus Perceiving

While the previous two dimensions, Sensing versus Intuition and Thinking versus Feeling, are referred to as mental functions, this final dimension is usually described as an *orientation* to the outside world. This dimension was not developed by Carl Jung but was developed as an addition to his theory by Isabel Briggs Myers and her mother, Katharine Briggs.

Those who prefer Judging are people who like to have life under control. They naturally tend to make decisions and seek closure, and doing so makes them feel comfortable. Once they have enough information to make a decision, they like to make it and close the issue. They are natural planners who prefer structure and organization in the way they both live and work. At work they are the ones who are most comfortable with a clear-desk policy, since they like to take action, complete the task, and file jobs as soon as possible. In a couple, the one with the strongest preference for Judging is the partner who has planned the weekend in advance, the holiday suitcases and other arrangements all in hand. This type probably goes shopping with a list. Judging types are decisive and organized. If that does not sound like you, then perhaps you identify more closely with the characteristics of the Perceiving type.

Perceiving types prefer to be flexible and spontaneous. If there is no pressing need to make a decision, then why make one? Far better to continue to gather information and keep all options open until you are forced to close them. After all, surely the more information you have and the better informed you are, the better the ultimate decision? Perceiving types seek to understand life rather than control it. Booking dates in a day planner (if they have one) can make them feel slightly depressed because they much prefer to keep the future open and be ready to take advantage of new opportunities that arise. Clear-desk policies are seen as Judging-type imperialism—why file something if it is still waiting to be closed out? Judging types also complain because Perceiving types cannot provide a progress report on their current work and because, although they always hit the required deadlines, they always do so at the last minute. Perceiving types can counter by reminding Judging types of the urgent jobs that the Perceiving types always seem to pick up because the day planners of the former are always fully booked. It is very important for Perceiving types to feel their options are open. They prefer the freedom of being able to go with the flow, trusting their ability to adapt to new situations as they arise. They thrive on the adrenaline of meeting deadlines just in time. Sometimes it seems that they even delay starting a project just to let the pressure build.

I once ran a predeparture program for a young married couple who had accepted an overseas posting. As part of their preparation, I suggested that they both take the Myers-Briggs Type Indicator. After completing the questionnaire, I gave them both an individual feedback session, at the end of which it was established that they both had the same type preferences and that they both had a clear preference for Judging. This did not really surprise me as their preparation, even prior to the program, had been well thought out and meticulous. Later in the day they shared their type preferences with each other. At first they were both delighted at being so similar, but then they began to think about what this meant in terms of their overseas posting. From their previous experience, they knew that they worked well together in organizing the logistical side of travel, both before setting out and later in being able to quickly establish routines and some sort of order on arrival. They both agreed that they were not so good at dealing with the unexpected problems that travel always seemed to produce, such as the sudden requirement of an official document, a delayed travel connection, or someone responding in a totally unexpected way. As they discussed this, it quickly became apparent to them that raising this as a possible issue was in itself reassuring and useful to them. They could now adjust their planning to include some flexibility, not just in their logistical arrangements but also in their own thinking about what could be planned for and controlled, and what could not.

In terms of cross-cultural effectiveness, both dimensions are useful in meeting quite different demands, since like all the other dimensions, the two are diametrically opposed; if you are in one, then you are clearly not in the other. I personally have a very clear preference for Perceiving, so when I am traveling, I like to have a very flexible itinerary or, better still, no itinerary at all. However, to allow myself greater freedom, flexibility, and mobility in situ, I use Judging type thinking to plan what I will be likely to need en route and to pack carefully and economically so I can carry everything in a single small bag. My Perceiving preference enables me to enjoy going with the flow and to stay open to new experiences, which in turn helps me to take unexpected obstacles in stride without getting upset or stressed by them. My Judging preference comes into play when schedules must be arranged and met, when detailed plans must be made, or when it is time to fall into a routine of packing and moving on.

Myers-Briggs Type Theory Expanded

So far, all I have provided is a brief description of the basic scales within the Myers-Briggs Type Indicator model and one or two examples, out of a potentially limitless range, of how each preference may be called into play in a typical cross-cultural situation. If I were to leave you with the impression that each of these dimensions is discrete and separate from the others, then I would not have done justice to the model at all. In order to realize the true potential of the model, it is necessary to see how the distinct processes work together to make up the whole, just as our senses work in unison to provide us with a depth of experience.

Type theory dynamics is the key to understanding type at a deeper level; it expands the two-dimensional model I have described so far into a richer three-dimensional model. Understanding the order in which you prefer to use your functions is the key to type dynamics. In much the same way that we are born with a preference for being right- or left-handed, each person has an innate preference for one of the four mental functions (Sensing/Intuition, the two perceiving functions, or Thinking/Feeling, the two decision-making functions), and this preference develops into the *dominant function*. How you use your dominant function will depend on whether you are oriented toward Extraversion or Introversion. For example, an extravert who has Intuition as a dominant function will use it in an extraverted way, bouncing ideas off other people, networking, discussing new plans, and so on. Others will regard her as someone who is good at seeing possibilities and the big picture, someone who can be relied upon to generate new ideas. An introvert with Intuition as his dominant function may not be recognized by others as having the qualities just mentioned simply because her intuition takes place inside her head, and she does not have the same drive to share her intuiting with others.

The function that follows the dominant is referred to as the *auxiliary function*. If your dominant function is Perceiving, then the auxiliary will be a decision-making function or vice versa. For example, if your dominant function is Feeling, which is a decision-making function, your auxiliary must be one of the Perceiving functions, that is, either Sensing or Intuition.

The function that follows the auxiliary function is referred to as the *tertiary* or *third function*. If your auxiliary is a Perceiving function, then your tertiary will be the other Perceiving function; if it is a decision-making function, then your tertiary will be the other decision-making function. So if your auxiliary preference is Sensing, your tertiary preference must be Intuition and vice versa.

Your fourth and least-preferred function is referred to as your *inferior function*. If your dominant function is one of the decision-making functions, then your least-preferred function will also be a decision-making function. For example, if your dominant function is Feeling, your inferior function will be Thinking and vice versa. If your dominant function is Intuition, your inferior will be Sensing and vice versa. This is because you naturally spend a large proportion of your time using your dominant function and because the functions in each dimension are diametrically opposed (you cannot make decisions using both your Feeling and Thinking functions simultaneously). Thus, if Feeling is your dominant and most-used function, then Thinking must be your inferior and least-used function.

Travel and dealing with cross-cultural interactions cause pressure and stress. Different people will view and respond to the same situation in different ways. To manage cross-cultural relationships and change effectively, you must first understand yourself and what impact you have on others; this is where the MBTI comes in handy. Under physical and/or psychological pressure, we tend to default to particular behaviors, usually relying heavily on our dominant function to solve whatever problems we face. However, when the pressure is more than even our dominant function can deal with, then our least-preferred, or inferior, function can assume temporary control. When this occurs we appear to be "not ourselves" and to others our behavior may seem irrational, even a little crazy. Remember that your inferior function is the one that is the least used, and therefore the least developed.

My inferior or least-developed function is Thinking, which is a decision-making function. Normally, given the choice, I make decisions on a largely subjective basis, using logic only when it is clearly required. When I am under a lot of stress my Thinking function has on occasion assumed temporary command. The combination of stress combined with operating from my least-preferred function is alarming not only to me but possibly to those around me as well. A decision made by someone with a preference for Thinking is normally a rational decision based on a logical, pragmatic, and objective consideration of all the data, including any emotional inputs. However, a Thinking-based decision made by someone under stress whose least-preferred function is Thinking is a recipe for some irrational and out-of-character behavior. For a dominant Feeling type who is generally known as a friendly, easygoing people person, the result could be illogical judgments about his own competence, sarcastic and even aggressive criticism of those closest to him, and unexpected precipitous action. In short, the opposite of what you would normally expect from that person.

I sometimes find that I come to illogical conclusions and judgments that others find surprising. On one occasion I was feeling under strain and had a training course to run. After the course had finished, I noticed that one of the participants had completed a course evaluation form that rated my performance as average. When I read it, I immediately overreacted, first with anger against the perpetrator (just as well he was not around) and then against myself and my own competence as a trainer. A surprising and illogical reaction, since all the other returned evaluation forms contained positive statements. Thankfully it did not take long for my other functions to reassert themselves and put things back into perspective. Later I looked back and wondered why I had reacted in the way I had.

At other times, my least-preferred function of Thinking has come to my aid. When I have felt overwhelmed with the sheer mass of tasks facing me, my logical function has helped me to consider the pros and cons of doing each task and to prioritize my work and domestic life accordingly. I have also noticed that once the panic is past, I revert to my happy-go-lucky approach to planning. The time manager is quietly put to rest again in my desk drawer.

Cross-cultural effectiveness begins with understanding yourself. Understanding how and why you react in a particular way when under stress will help you plan and ultimately cope better with the challenges you will undoubtedly encounter as you travel and interact. I suspect that a clear link could be made between a person's MBTI type and how they react to culture shock and stress brought on by the challenges of travel and of crossing cultural boundaries.

Those whose dominant function is extraverted Sensing often suffer from internal confusion under stress and from assigning the wrong meaning to events going on around them. They may find that Intuition is in the driver's seat for a while. Useful Intuition is about seeing the big picture and being drawn toward future possibilities. However, in its undeveloped and capricious form, the possibilities it offers may be either grandiose promises or catastrophes waiting to happen.

Those whose dominant function is extroverted Intuition are likely to become withdrawn and depressed under stress, and with their least-favored Sensing function in the driver's seat, their attention is on sensory information and detail. However, this may take the form of obsessive behavior and a focus on their own body and its well-being.

For dominant extraverted Thinking types, who are normally rational, objective, and logical, stress can bring the Feeling function to the surface, and the result can be unexpected and out-of-character outbursts of emotion. They may experience a fear of feeling, a reluctance to deal with their own emotions, and be hypersensitive to their inner state.

For dominant extraverted Feeling types, the change when their inferior Thinking function takes temporary command is equally dramatic. The undeveloped Thinking function generates convoluted logic and a compulsive search for truth. Those around them may be surprised at the criticism suddenly leveled at them from someone they had always known as warm and friendly.

With every permutation of functions, a different reaction to stress is likely, from overindulgence to withdrawal and depression, from obsessive attention to detail to the anticipation of grandiose and catastrophic possibilities, from convoluted logic to emotional outbursts. Usually, with the right assistance or a bit of time, the natural order of a person's functions reasserts itself and the person reverts to her normal self.

For the traveler, or indeed for anyone who is trying to build intercultural relationships, it is important to be able to recognize the early signs of stress and know how your behavior tends to change when you are under stress. You can then take action to minimize the impact of your behavior while "in the grip" so that you do not do something you regret later, or that irretrievably spoils the relationships you are trying to build. I am talking about damage limitation. If, for example, you feel that you are likely to verbally attack someone, then try to avoid those situations that will present opportunities to do so, at least until you feel yourself regaining more control. On the other hand, if your normal response to stress is to withdraw into depression and distance yourself from others, then at least make the decision and the effort to maintain an acceptable, albeit minimum, level of cordiality with those around you. All human beings around the world have problems and usually can accept them in others. If you do act out of character in a way you later regret, usually your best policy is to simply apologize for the behavior and sincerely try to make amends.

The following three stress response characteristics are common to all personality types.

1. *Anger.* The form the anger will take and how it is expressed will depend on the function driving it.
2. *Tunnel vision.* Under stress, all types have an irrational focus on one thing or some aspect of their situation to the exclusion of all other possibilities and suggestions.
3. *Loss of sense of humor.* To understand humor requires the ability to see things in a wider perspective. Under stress, the vision narrows and any sense of humor tends to disappear.

If you recognize these symptoms in yourself or in those around you, remember—once in this state, the last thing people want is for someone to make fun of anything, to reason with them, to contradict them, to argue, or for you to defend yourself from any of their criticisms or accusations. What is required is empathy—validation of the sufferer's concerns and reassurance that their problems are taken seriously.

In-depth coverage of the stress response, examples of how stress can be triggered, and the form stress may take in different types is covered in Naomi L. Quenk's excellent book, *Beside Ourselves* (1993).

Type Differences and Culture

The Myers-Briggs Type Indicator questionnaire has been successfully translated into many languages and used around the world. Carl Jung, Isabel Myers, and Katharine Briggs believed that the dimensions they had identified were universal and common to all humans, and research to date supports their belief. Given that type differences are universal, how the differences are expressed within the context of a national culture will obviously differ, depending on individual cultural background. An extraverted Finnish man in the U.K. may not, on the surface, exhibit many characteristics usually associated with extraversion in the U.K. In his home culture, however, his extraverted preference would probably be more apparent, relative to other

Finns. Most people from Britain would probably consider that on average the ratio of extraverts to introverts is higher in the United States than in Britain. However, the available statistics show the opposite is true. No doubt our perception of what is considered extraverted and introverted behavior is relative to how the behavior is displayed in our own culture. For instance, the U.S. education system teaches children from a young age to be able to stand up and present themselves in a way that makes them appear outgoing and confident compared with their U.K. counterparts.

It has been found, however, that the use of the MBTI may not be appropriate in cultures with a strong group orientation, where the interests of the group tend to prevail over the interests of the individual. The importance of the group is central to individuals within it. As a result, individuals may first see themselves as part of a continent, a nation, a tribe, a clan, or an extended family and only last as distinct individuals, which makes it difficult for them to identify and report on their individual preferences. Moreover, in strongly group-oriented cultures the way type is expressed, particularly with regard to Introversion, may be significantly different from how it is expressed in more individualistic cultures. The items on the MBTI questionnaire may not, as a result, tap into group-oriented introverts' experience of how they process information internally.

It is tempting to try to align the four Myers-Briggs dimensions with dimensions of cultural difference of the sort that I will describe later in the book. For example, we might want to align

- Feeling types with those cultures whose focus is more on the relationship than the task,
- Thinking types with those cultures that are task focused and logical,
- Judging types with cultures that display high levels of structure and precision,
- Perceiving types with those cultures where everything can be put off until tomorrow,
- Sensing types with those cultures famous for practical and functional construction, and
- Intuitive types with those cultures renowned for invention and innovation.

What would this exercise tell us? Could we really assume that just because someone has a dominant function for Feeling that they could never prefer the efficiency and privacy offered by a task-focused culture? That the dominant Thinking type could not be enchanted and at ease enjoying the sense of belonging they could enjoy in a group-oriented culture? Frameworks of cultural difference, as we shall see, are attempts to provide insight into how cultures compare when measured against some universal human problem. The Myers-Briggs Type Indicator does not set out to measure anything. Effectively, it is trying to establish for the taker a profile of preferences that reflect his or her natural choices.

All cultures of the world contain their share of all the Myers-Briggs types, and each culture influences how people within the culture express their type. *People are born with their MBTI preferences,* and they continue to develop them throughout life. A person's cultural programming is acquired by being brought up in a particular culture. If you take a young baby from a culture into which it has just been born and raise it in a different culture, the child will acquire the cultural values of the second culture, but its type preferences will remain unchanged. When people of the same type, but from very different cultures, are grouped together to exchange views in workshops, they are often surprised at how similar their views are and at the many common experiences they share.

As we have now seen, type differences are more complex than the characteristics associated with each preference. It is the interaction among the preferences that is the key to understanding type at a deeper level. I hope this brief introduction to the Myers-Briggs Type Indicator has whetted your appetite and shown you how it can help you understand personality differences in a more structured way. If you are interested in taking the Myers-Briggs Type Indicator yourself, see the address and contact details at the end of the References.

What Is Your Boiling Point?

Several years ago when I was in Madras, India, I was speaking to the owner of a small hotel when we were disturbed by a commotion outside. We both went to the door and were met by the following spectacle. Two backpackers, built on the large side, were both squeezed into the back of a hand-drawn rickshaw along with their equally large packs. They were haranguing the rickshaw driver, a gaunt Indian man, who was soaked in perspiration and breathing heavily from dragging them through the roads in the center of the City of Madras. I retreated back into to the shade of the hotel foyer along with the owner; haggling over a price was such a commonplace event it did not merit our attention. However, minutes later, the pitch and tone of the exchange changed; we now heard loud accusatory shouts from the intrepid travelers and equally loud responses from the driver. "Do you want us to fetch the police right now?" one of the backpackers screamed, his finger pointing in the face of the driver. By now, both the travelers were sweating as heavily as the driver, who stood his ground defiantly facing the two men, his hand outstretched to receive the fare that wasn't coming.

The hotel owner finally walked over to the group. He had the diplomatic skills the situation required, and besides, heated confrontations on his doorstep were not good for business. Within moments I saw the backpackers grudgingly part with some rupees and the driver pick up the handles of his rickshaw and move off into the traffic, his head shaking and his expression heavy with contempt. After the two backpackers had checked in and gone to their rooms, the owner told me that the dispute had indeed been the result of a misunderstanding over the fare. However, when he then told me what the difference was—what the driver had demanded and what the backpackers had thought they should pay—I was amazed. "But that only amounts to two pence in English money!" I exclaimed. The owner inclined his head slightly. "Quite so," he replied, without judgment.

Clearly, those rupees had more value to the driver than to the travelers. I will let you make up your own minds about the ethics of the situation. However, what intrigued me about the incident was that it illustrated so clearly how easy it is to lose perspective, to get worked up and stressed out, defending something that is just not worth it. You know how often and how easily you get wound up. Clearly, some people have a lower threshold than others.

From A to B

Meyer Friedman and Ray H. Rosenman (1975) created the Type A and Type B distinctions of behavior, which provide a useful way of gauging whether your threshold is likely to be high or low, along with many other tendencies. Look down the following lists and see which type best describes you.

Typical behavior for a *Type A* person:

- Trying to do more things in less time
- Task driven
- A tendency to suppress fatigue
- Extreme competitiveness

- Unrealistic urgency
- Inappropriate ambition
- A reluctance to reflect on himself
- A strong need for control

Typical behavior for a *Type B* person:

- Unhurried and patient
- A relaxed, easy-going approach to life
- Focus on quality of life rather than quantity of output or achievement
- Low competitiveness
- Tolerant and friendly
- A tendency for self-reflection

According to this typology, those readers who recognize themselves as Type A are more likely to concentrate on tasks and feel driven to achieve goals when on an overseas posting and to have less patience with the cross-cultural diversions and interruptions that threaten their effectiveness. Earlier in the book I gave three criteria for measuring a successful cross-cultural journey or posting:

1. The traveler feels comfortable and at ease in her new environment. After allowing for a reasonable period of adjustment, which is needed for any major life change, she has a general sense of well-being and feels that her time in this new environment is time well spent.

2. The sojourner has the interpersonal resources to enable her to overcome obstacles, operate successfully in the new culture, and complete her tasks or projects. Many expatriates, and certainly development workers, understand that project success is not simply completing a task; success also involves skills and knowledge transfer to the host nationals.

3. Members of the host culture feel comfortable with the traveler and enjoy her company. The traveler has the ability to develop warm and cordial relationships with people from within the host culture. She also participates in the everyday activities of the host culture and has a visible respect for those activities. Once established in the host country, the visitor may look forward to signs of her acceptance into the host culture, possibly signaled by personal invitations to a local's

home or to functions such as weddings, funerals, christening ceremonies, and parties. In the workplace, acceptance may be signaled by the unsolicited sharing of information, information that normally would not be shared with an outsider and certainly not with someone local work colleagues did not trust.

Type A characteristics are often useful in task effectiveness. However, they are usually not conducive to building close relationships, which often requires Type B characteristics, such as patience, perception, tolerance, reflection, and sensitivity.

At this stage those of you who recognize yourself as more Type A than Type B may be starting to feel that you have been stuck with a rigid and negative label and thus stereotyped in the worst possible way. Allow me to repackage Friedman and Rosenman's theory a bit differently.

Rather than seeing two personality types, either A or B, I prefer to see two sets of tendencies and characteristics, shared by all people, that surface in varying degrees given different contexts and situations. For example, perhaps my two backpackers in Madras were jet-lagged and tired, perhaps something else had happened that added to their level of stress, and at a different time or on a different day they might have reacted completely differently. However, some people's behavior generally leans more toward the Type A characteristics, while others, on average, tend more toward the Type B characteristics. Looked at in this way, the labels lose their rigidity and become indicators on a sliding scale rather than name tags or labels. In addition, people who find that their own habits of behavior do not always serve them well have the choice of changing them. This is a theme that I will repeat throughout this book.

Stephen Covey, in his book *The Seven Habits of Highly Effective People* (1989), refers to the pause between a stimulus and your response to it. In other words, if something happens, you have the freedom to choose how to react. Even if you have become conditioned to behave or react in a certain way to a given set of circumstances, why not change your response if you find that your habitual response is not serving you well? Even if you identify strongly with Type A characteristics, you can still choose to pause before reacting in your usual way and to select a more effective response. Remember, not everything in life benefits from being done quickly.

Of course, for most people, changing habitual behavior is not easy. Their natural response may not even be in the form of behavior that is visible to others but in the way they feel about the stimulus. If you accept that you have a choice in how you respond to situations and would like to replace some habitual behavior with more appropriate responses, then the next two sections, "Conscious Inhibition" and "State Interrupts," should help get you started.

Conscious Inhibition

Conscious inhibition is not the sort of inhibition found in Freudian textbooks, which is linked to holding back feelings. I am referring here to the inhibition of our immediate physical response to a stimulus. This technique forms part of the training for those being instructed in the Alexander Technique (Alexander 1987). The Alexander Technique is in fact a method of becoming more aware of ourselves and of how we use our bodies on a daily basis. In particular it enables us, with the aid of a suitably qualified teacher, to become aware of habitual behavior that is harmful to posture and therefore to our bodies. Alexander used the example of a cat to illustrate what he meant by inhibition. When a cat first spots a mouse, it does not immediately rush forward and pounce on it, but waits instead for the right moment when it is most likely to be successful in catching its prey.

Conscious inhibition has nothing to do with suppression; it is about consciously delaying, so that we have the freedom to choose the most appropriate response to a given situation and to execute it most effectively. Some time back I was suffering aching hands from typing on a computer keyboard. A member of the medical health department checked my typing posture and style and realized that not only was my work station set up all wrong, but my typing style and posture were also poor. My typing style and posture seemed comfortable and natural to me—bad habits often do! In fact, my posture was the main cause of my tendinitis. I was shown the correct posture and how my hands and arms should be placed in relation to the keyboard. For some time afterward, however, I had to consciously pause and physically stop myself from reverting to my old habits.

The ability to consciously pause before reacting is useful in cross-cultural encounters, particularly when you are interacting with people you are meeting for the first time. In these situations, you are often being watched very closely, and how you react to what you see and hear is noted. For example, local hospitality may dictate that you are offered a plate of food on arrival. Let us say that your immediate reaction to the food is one of distaste or even revulsion. You can immediately communicate to the hosts what you think of their offering with grimaces and other body language. Or, you can suspend any judgments on the food, courteously accept the offering, and just not eat it.

In the first instance you are concerned only for yourself; in the second you are showing concern for the host's feelings and reputation. Of course, you could show even greater concern by actually eating a little bit of the food as well! Who knows? It might taste better than it looks. The key is being able to pause before you react. This is especially important when locals invite you into their homes, when people describe features of their lifestyle and culture, when attending important local ceremonies and rituals, at formal occasions steeped in official protocol, and similar situations requiring sensitivity.

You can apply this concept to inappropriate Type A behavior. After first identifying those patterns of behavior that you want to change, you then make a voluntary and conscious decision that you no longer want to respond in your current habitual way. You are now consciously aware of the behavior you want to change. The next time you find yourself in a situation where you are about to slip into your usual inappropriate behavior, you will be reminded to pause and think of an alternative and more appropriate response.

State Interrupts

State interrupts are useful when you find yourself in a mental or emotional state that does not benefit you and that you want to change or snap out of. A *state* is the sum total of what you are thinking and feeling at a moment in time. For example, you could be in a state of ecstasy, terror, rage, confusion, panic, and so on. Moving in and out of different states throughout the day is normal and usually is no cause for concern. The state could, for example, be one you choose to remain in, such as a state of well-being. Some states, however, can be overwhelming and prevent you from functioning rationally. Such states are uncomfortable, debilitating, and difficult to shake off. For two reasons, such states can be disastrous for the sojourner. First, in another country you are among people who have limited experience of your normal temperament, so if you suddenly behave irrationally or aggressively the host nationals may assume that they are seeing another inherent and perhaps rather unpleasant side of you, whereas family and friends back home would see your behavior as uncharacteristic. The second reason relates to the discussion in Chapter 1: When traveling abroad, you often have to rely on yourself to solve problems, and losing control of yourself, particularly in an emergency, can leave you very vulnerable indeed.

As a young teenager I once found myself in a state of panic on my first long trip alone. Arriving at my destination early in the morning, I ate in a local café, paid the bill, and walked leisurely out into the sunshine and into the market square. I felt a tremendous sense of calm and well-being that lasted for all of five minutes, until I reached inside my shirt to check that my passport and money were still there—they weren't. My calm state instantly changed to one of blind panic. Feeling suddenly a little dizzy, I felt myself starting to hyperventilate. I was on the point of rushing around the market and searching for them on the ground when, with some effort, I managed to break out of the state for a moment. It was only then that I remembered the café—I had them in the café! Rushing back, I saw the owner waiting for me with my passport and money in his hand. My state was now one of relief and joy and, of course, immense gratitude to the honest café owner. The ability to break out of a state that is preventing you from functioning in the way you need to is an extremely useful skill.

The term *state interrupt* comes from the field of Neuro-Linguistic Programming, which I referred to in Chapter 2 earlier in the book. (Suggestions for further reading are also provided in the References.) In order to have some control over a state, normally an unconscious process, we first need to develop a conscious awareness of ourselves and to be able to notice what state we are in at any given time.

We internally represent, or experience, whatever state we are in through images we remember or construct in our heads—through values, beliefs, feelings, and decisions and even through our physiology. If we alter any of these components, we can also alter or interrupt the state. For example, if you are in a state of anxiety because you are on an aircraft and have a fear of flying, you may realize that you are internally creating mental images of all the disasters that could conceivably happen to a plane. Playing around with the images in your head (yes, this is possible; it's your brain after all) will alter the state you are in. Try changing them to black and white, fade the contrast out, make the images smaller, turn the images into surreal caricatures so that the plane resembles a big yellow banana and all the passengers are in cartoon-style fancy dress.

If your state is one of low self-esteem or confidence, which you represent internally with a nagging "I told you so" type of voice that keeps telling you that you are a failure, then change the voice for a squeaky comic voice that you find impossible to take seriously. Or try overriding the voice with another internal voice, maybe a parade ground sergeant who can shout the other person down. Simply thinking of something completely different will achieve a change in your state. Have you ever seen someone sitting alone, relaxed and smiling, and when you ask why they are so happy, they tell you that they were just remembering their holidays, or a night out, or a good weekend? Their memories had changed their mental and physical state; this is connected to the same principle I emphasize here. Changing your physiology—for example, your posture—can effect an emotional change. If you put yourself into an assertive posture, then you are more likely to be able to behave in an assertive way.

Doing almost anything strange, new, different, oddball, or surprising will interrupt a state, and a really effective interrupt will jar the negative state so it cannot continue. Try to find an interrupt that works effectively for you. In fact, develop some additional interrupts that cover different senses, some that you can access without anyone else being aware of it, and maybe some more overt interrupts that entail a physical movement, a sign, or a change of posture.

Once again, all this may sound strange, but please suspend judgment until you have tried it out—it really does work.

Self-Awareness and Feelings

The state that we are in at any waking moment is a result of our thinking, feeling, and behavior. Think back to the last time you were caught in the grip of a strong emotion like anger, guilt, hate, or grief, and try to remember what you actually did. Did you react and express what you were feeling at the time, possibly with an angry retort or with sarcasm, or did you suppress your feelings, forcing your body to absorb or discharge the negative energy as best it could? It probably felt at the time that either your feelings were controlling you or you were so clenched up inside, your feelings almost seemed a physical part of you. *There is a crucial difference between being swept along by your emotions and feelings unconsciously and being consciously aware that you are being swept along by them.* In the latter case, you are being self-aware in that you are recognizing your feelings as they occur. When you do this, you are more likely to be able to maintain some control.

Some people are able to do this more easily than others, but it is a technique that most people can improve on if they work at it. Practice by monitoring your state during the day—how stressed or relaxed you feel, how annoyed or calm. Having identified the state, accept it mentally, perhaps by saying to yourself something like, "Their behavior has annoyed me so much I am tense and wound up." Next, ask yourself what course of action is best to maintain or reach the state you want to be in.

For example, a sojourner abroad may consider the local system of giving some sort of payment to a public official in order to "persuade" him to sign a perfectly legitimate document as an immoral way of working, and so at odds with her values that she goes into a rage just thinking about it. Apart from leaving the country or beginning a solo crusade against the country's immoral (at least by her standards) public servants, what is she to do? Although her rage may be a useful motivation if she chooses the solo crusade option, it is certainly not helpful if she does not. First, she needs to acknowledge that she is angry, what the focus of her anger is, and what about it makes her so angry. Just thinking through these points, if done in a rational and objective manner, may calm her down. Then she could try to view the system from a local's point of view. This may not lead her to approve of or even like the system any more, but at least she will have broadened her understanding and lowered her blood pressure.

Feelings do not exist in a physical form, and you can choose how much or how little impact they will have on you. In fact, the only person who is stopping you from letting go and releasing those uncomfortable feelings is yourself.

Try this little exercise. Think back to an issue over which you still hold strong feelings, and access those feelings now. Once you have them, where do the feelings appear to be physically located—your stomach or chest, for instance? What sensations accompany the feelings in those locations—clenched, heavy? Now allow yourself to breathe deeply and consciously relax the areas in question, in much the same way that you would let go of a coin that you had been gripping tightly. At first there is a reluctance to let go, but once you make a focused and conscious effort, the hand opens and the coin falls to the ground. The issue that generated the feelings may still be there, but you can now review it with more objectivity and deal with it, or not, as you decide.

Accepting that we are holding on to particular feelings and then making a conscious decision to release them is something many of us never do. If something annoys you and you fail to do something about it, then the negative feelings and energy can persist. Sometimes just recognizing the state you are in as it occurs can lead you to more useful thinking about what you should do.

There will be occasions when you genuinely do not want to let go of particular feelings, which is okay as well; just accept that you are uncomfortable or upset and let the feelings be. Often, acceptance achieves much the same result as letting go of a feeling. In some instances it seems you need to pass through a stage of denial before you can move forward to the next stage of acceptance.

Understand Your Own Stress Response

Early in the book I described how important it is to ensure that your communication is congruent, that your tonality and nonverbal behavior support your spoken message. Incongruent communication can arise when you show nervous tension, not because of the message you are giving, but because of the circumstances or context in which you are delivering the message. For example, you might be nervous about meeting a person for the first time, being alone in a foreign country, the pressure from headquarters to succeed with an important negotiation, or simply a lack of time. It is at times like these that you really need to be able to control the state you are in so that you can focus on the situation at hand. All too often it is the state that controls us. Remember my anecdote about my lost passport and money, and how I said I felt dizzy and had started to hyperventilate? Have you ever experienced panic physically? Perhaps you have suffered some of these symptoms when nervous:

- Faster heartbeat
- Dry mouth
- Blushing, going red or pale
- Shaking
- Higher pitch in your speech
- Loss of normal vocabulary
- Breathlessness, shallow breathing in upper chest
- The need to go to the toilet
- Butterflies in your stomach
- Your mind going blank

- Light-headedness, feeling faint
- Nausea
- Constriction in your throat; tension around your head, neck, and shoulders

When the classic symptoms of the fight-or-flight stress response kick in, it seems as if your own body is trying to undermine and embarrass you. In fact, your body is really trying its best to help you; the problem is, it has the message wrong. When your brain senses anxiety, your body is programmed to respond in one way—to prepare you to meet a physical threat. This is great in those hopefully rare occasions when your safety or life is indeed threatened but inappropriate when the situation is simply one where you need to be calm, relaxed, and in command of yourself.

In order to control your stress response, it is useful to have a basic understanding of how the stress response operates. There are three separate but interdependent nervous systems in the body:

1. The *central nervous system*
   - Controls all voluntary actions
   - Controls conscious sensations such as taste, sight, hearing, smell, muscular contractions, and the experience of internal pain and injury
2. The *parasympathetic nervous system*
   - Controls the digestive tract and the production of digestive juices
   - Controls the involuntary movement of stomach and bowels for digestion and defecation
   - Both balances and opposes the sympathetic nervous system
3. The *sympathetic nervous system*
   - Influences the entire body by monitoring blood pressure, blood chemistry, and repair
   - Is responsible for your body's built-in autonomic stress response

All the symptoms of nervousness and anxiety I described earlier can be explained when we examine what happens to our nervous systems when we experience anxiety.

Symptom/Physical State	Cause/Your Body's Response
Faster heartbeat	The adrenaline coursing through your bloodstream has triggered your heart to work faster in anticipation of physical exertion.
Dry mouth	When the sympathetic nervous system takes command, other functions are closed off temporarily as your inner resources are diverted toward the major muscle groups that may be called upon to help you fight or run away.
Blushing, going red or pale	You body is anticipating that very soon you will be engaged in violent activity and likely get very hot, so it has started one of the biological functions that will help you lose heat. Sending blood to the fine capillaries on the surface of the skin is an effective cooling mechanism. Tension around the head, neck, and shoulders, however, can reduce the blood supply in some areas, which will appear pale in comparison. In addition, the main supply of blood is being redirected to areas where it is most needed, such as the leg muscles and brain.
Shaking	The intermittent tightening and releasing of muscles that causes the "shakes" is nature's way of warming up the muscles so they are ready for action. It is also easier to react quickly with movement when your body is already in motion.
Higher pitch in your speech	Muscular tension in your body in general and around your neck in particular will change the quality of your voice. Speaking requires three basic ingredients: a blast of air from the lungs, vocal chords to vibrate and produce the sound, and resonating chambers to amplify the sound. The

resonating chambers include the mouth, throat, sinuses, and some other cavities around the upper body. Nervous tension that causes muscle tension will have the effect of constricting the size of the resonating chambers and the flow of air over the vocal chords. The voice will subsequently lose resonance and richness and will sound reedy and high.

Loss of normal vocabulary
In survival situations, the brain will normally operate at a more primitive level. Running from danger or fighting for your life does not require eloquence. As your body marshals its resources to meet the threat, vocabulary is low on its list of priorities.

Breathlessness, shallow breathing in upper chest
When we are under stress our solar plexus, which is situated just under the diaphragm, clenches into a knot. The diaphragm is forced up, forcing us to breathe a reduced quantity of air in our upper chest.

The need to go to the toilet
The sympathetic and parasympathetic nervous systems work in opposition to each other. Under normal conditions, if one of the systems is stimulated then the other almost switches off. The parasympathetic nervous system controls the digestive tract and the stomach. In situations that make you nervous, it is usual to feel a need to use the toilet. This is nature's way of helping you to shed weight prior to flight or fight. Defecation has also been recognized as a bodily function that lowers our stress level, albeit temporarily.

Butterflies in your stomach
Also caused by the effect on the digestive tract as described above.

Your mind going blank	Same reason as for loss of vocabulary.
Light-headedness, feeling faint	Constriction of a ring of muscle around the back of the neck can lead to a reduction in the supply of blood to the head and brain and result in a feeling of light-headedness and faintness.
Nausea	Same as the need to use the toilet.
Constriction in your throat; tension around your head, neck, and shoulders	Tension of the muscles surrounding vulnerable areas of the body is one of the body's defense mechanisms to protect us from blows and help make us more compact and thus a smaller target.

Knowing two facts will help you control your stress response. First, your subconscious stress response cannot distinguish between a real and an imagined threat. For example, many travelers feel uneasy as they pass through customs checks, even though they are carrying no contraband and have never had problems with customs officials in the past. As they walk past the officials they may experience some of the classic stress response symptoms.

These imaginary threats can stem from something that we did or that happened to us many years earlier. When I was at school, I was a member of the local athletic club and represented my town at weekend races. I always felt nervous, with lots of adrenaline at the start of a race, which served me well during the race itself. More than thirty years later, when watching the start of a hundred-meter race on television while relaxing in an armchair, I still experience a tingling wave of the same feelings. Thrillers and horror films can have the same effect, even though the threat is clearly not a real one. We will pick up on this fact when we cover how to anchor a positive state.

Second, the sympathetic and parasympathetic nervous systems work in opposition and are balanced against one another. When one nervous system is stimulated, the other almost switches off. Thus, if you can somehow suppress your sympathetic response, the parasympathetic system will start to kick back in again, and you will be able to suppress or even neutralize the symptoms just listed. On the other hand, if you allow the sympathetic stress response to run unchecked, the symptoms will tend to escalate. Take those travelers who feel ill at ease when passing through customs checks. If they only focused on what it would be like to be stopped and arrested by customs officials for some reason, instead of rationally accepting that they have no cause for concern, then their mild stress response symptoms could escalate into full-blown fear, and no doubt prompt the customs officials to wonder what was causing the traveler to be so anxious.

Two Techniques for Controlling Your Stress Response

Two effective techniques for controlling your stress response are diaphragm breathing and anchoring a positive state. The aim of both these techniques is to activate your parasympathetic nervous system so that the sympathetic stress response is subdued or even switched off.

Diaphragm Breathing

We are often advised to take a deep breath to allay nerves, but additional advice on how to go about taking a deep breath usually fails to accompany the suggestion. This may seem like a banal statement; after all, who needs to be told how to breathe deeply? But think how you breathe when you are under stress. The common symptoms I listed arising from the activation of the sympathetic nervous system include rapid, shallow breathing in the upper chest. Doing more of the same or taking even bigger breaths in the upper chest would simply push you further into the stress response symptoms you are trying to escape.

Taking a deep breath means exactly that. Try placing one hand on your lower abdomen and the other on your upper chest. Now take a deep breath and notice which hand moves outward—is it the upper hand, the lower hand, or both hands? If your lower hand is the only one moving outward, then congratulations, you are breathing from your diaphragm. When you are feeling stressed, try the same experiment again. Stress causes us all to take shallow breaths, which not only plunges us further into the stress response, it also impedes the proper oxygen/carbon dioxide exchange your body needs.

You may find it difficult to breathe from your diaphragm at first. If so, either practice using your hands as physical indicators to help you locate and direct your breathing or, alternatively, try imagining that you are inflating a small balloon or beach ball located behind your navel. Slowly fill it as if you were breathing directly into the balloon through your navel. Follow with a slow and controlled exhalation. The slow, controlled exhalation is the one that relaxes and de-stresses you. The deep inhalation is the one that reenergizes you. Simply learning and practicing this breathing technique will help prevent your stress response from escalating and eventually spiraling out of control. If our nervous customs crosser had started to breathe from her diaphragm at the first feelings of stress, she could have prevented the sympathetic response from escalating further. Stress specialists recommend that if you get into the habit of diaphragm breathing, even for a few minutes only twice a day (perhaps while sitting at your desk at work, for example), then your overall stress level will fall.

Anchoring a Positive State

Anchoring is the term used to describe a positive and conscious version of Pavlovian conditioning. Pavlov noted that salivation was one of the autonomic responses to food displayed by the dogs in his laboratory. He experimented by ringing a bell every time that he fed the dogs. Soon the dogs were salivating at the sound of the bell even if the food had not been brought. The ringing of the bell had become neurologically linked to food in the dog's brains and now triggered the same autonomic response as the food.

In humans, our visual, auditory, and olfactory physiology constantly get associated with a range of states of mind and emotions. For example, do you find that hearing certain songs or music can stimulate your memory to take you back to some moment in the past, a holiday perhaps? The smell of a certain perfume or maybe wood smoke can invoke sharp memories of people or events, even if they occurred in our early youth. When we are in a responsive state such as anger, fear, pain, ecstasy, or joy, other stimuli, such as scents, sounds, or tastes tend to become associated with the state at the time we are experiencing it. Such associated stimuli can subsequently trigger the same response again. For example, suppose you were unfortunate enough to be involved in a car accident where you were thrown heavily against the steering wheel, the accordioned hood trapping you in a state of semi-consciousness, slumped over the wheel with the car horn blaring. Thereafter, the blaring of a car horn might trigger the same emotional and physiological state you were in at the time of the accident, even though it was not the car horn that injured you, (it may even have been responsible for attracting aid to you more quickly) and in this instance, the danger is only imagined. Sojourners in the tropics who have put their foot into a shoe and been stung by a scorpion may find that they can never again put on a shoe without first turning it upside down and banging it on the floor to see if anything is inside, even though they no longer live a country that has indigenous scorpions.

The more intense the original experience, the stronger the connections any associated stimuli will have. So when you encounter the same stimuli, you will quickly find yourself in the same state again. Phobias are sometimes acquired in this way, often in a person's formative years, and therefore they are an example of a powerful association that in most cases was established in a single very brief but intense experience. If you have a phobia yourself, or know someone who does, then you realize that people never stop reacting to the connected stimulus. Just think how useful it would be if you could create a positive version of a phobia and access it whenever you wanted to.

In fact, it is possible to create such a positive association through anchoring. Basically, anchoring is a process that sets up an association between a chosen physiological and mental state and a discrete stimulus. Once the association has been made, then it is possible to access the state at will by simply using the chosen stimulus. First you choose the positive state that you would like to have access to; then you remember a time when you experienced that state. Where you were and what you were doing at the time are irrelevant to the process; what is crucial is that you were in the state that you want. It is the state, not the memory, that you are connecting to your chosen stimulus. This is how it is done.

Steps

1. Think of a state that would be useful to access for a particular situation you will face. For example, you might choose a state where you feel relaxed and confident. Even though I am suggesting that you use anchoring specifically to help you in cross-cultural situations, the state that you want to anchor can be from any time in your past. The important point is that you clearly remember the state that you were in at the time. A state recalled from a happy childhood day out in Wisconsin can be anchored via this process to help you control your state thirty years later in a foreign war zone.

2. Recall a time when you were in that state with all the resources that you identified in step one.

3. Next, decide what your associated stimuli or anchor will be; in other words, what discrete action will trigger your chosen state? To be most effective, I suggest that you use a combination of physical (for

example, squeezing your thumb and index finger together), auditory (imagine shouting an unusual, but memorable, word), and visual (see in your mind's eye a large billboard with the unusual word written on it in large letters) stimuli.

4. You are now ready to recall that moment in the past when you were in the chosen state. Recall the time as if you were there, reexperiencing what you saw, what you heard, and how you felt. If you find that you are watching yourself as if watching a film then you are not reexperiencing.

5. The best time to apply your chosen anchors is the moment just before you feel your recollection of that time is about to reach its peak. Anchoring the state as it is increasing in intensity sets a direction for the mind to follow.

6. Break your state by focusing your attention on something else. Get up and move around; look at an object in the room.

7. Repeat the above steps five or six times to build up a strong connection.

8. Test the anchors to see if they work. First, break the state again. Imagine the situation that you are preparing for and then use the anchors. Do they change your state into the desired state you want? If they do, then your setup has been successful; if not, repeat the process until you can access the required state whenever you want by activating the anchors you have established.

The more often you build, add to, and use your anchors, the quicker and easier you will be able to access them. If you experience another positive state at work, playing sports, or just relaxing, why not anchor it using the same triggers as before, so that it enriches the state already set up? Once they have been properly connected, your anchors will enable you to access the physiology quickly, without having to go through the process of remembering the original situations again each time. The physical trigger on its own becomes sufficient.

Once you have become adept at diaphragm breathing and anchoring, you will be able you to take control of your physical state rather than be controlled by it. As a result, in stressful cross-cultural situations you will send out fewer nonverbal messages of distress for your host to pick up and possibly misinterpret.

Getting to the Source of Your Stress

As you will have gathered, the techniques I have just described tackle the symptoms of stress response rather than its cause. The maxim "It is not things that upset people, but what people make of things" is certainly true. The philosopher Barthold Niebhur is credited with a similar statement: "It is not what happens to a person that most determines the person, but how he or she responds to that happening." The state that we are in inevitably reflects the meaning that we give to whatever we are focused on at that particular moment in time. L. Michael Hall (1996), in his book *Dragon Slaying*, identifies two "royal roads to state":

1. How we represent things internally to ourselves—visually, kinesthetically, auditorily; and how we speak to ourselves. It is through our beliefs, values, and understandings that we filter and give meaning to what we are experiencing, and
2. How we experience things externally through our physiology, posture, breathing, sense of well-being, biochemistry, and so forth.

Through these two interlinked routes our states emerge. What makes humans unique in the animal kingdom is our ability to think abstractly; for example, to think about ourselves as selves and to further reflect on what we have just thought. Reflecting and having thoughts about thoughts and feelings about feelings can quickly lead us up the Ladder of Inference that I referred to Chapter 2. Often this reflection has the effect of maintaining and magnifying the original state so that we stay in a state of stress response far longer than we should or need to.

Michael Hall refers to "canopies of consciousness." He describes how we can progress up through these canopies starting from the most primary, physical level at which we may experience calm, anger, joy, grief, or fear caused by an external source such as an event. Then as we think about the external event and how we feel about it, we attach additional meaning and so move to a higher level or canopy of consciousness. If we continue to reflect on the new meaning, we will have feelings about our feelings and attach still more meaning to the event and thus move to a still higher level or canopy of consciousness and so on. The highest level or canopy then determines how we feel and react to the earlier or lower canopies and to the external event.

Travel across cultural frontiers offers an endless supply of unfamiliar sensory stimuli. What state we are in as we meet these new stimuli will act as a filter for how we perceive and ascribe meaning to them. For example, if we arrive at a destination happy, optimistic, and upbeat, we will probably take a positive view of our surroundings, even if they are not what we had hoped they would be. At worst, we could take a philosophical stance and regard them as part of life's experience or as an adventure. If, on the other hand, our state upon arrival is one of pessimistic gloom, then our subsequent view of the same surroundings will be far more negative.

I have traveled in countries with high crime rates, but I always felt confident in the basic goodness of the majority of human beings. I am sure that many people would consider me naive for this belief. After more than twenty-five years of virtually theft- and violence-free travel (apart from a few incidents!), often in areas renowned for high crime rates, I continue to believe that being optimistic and holding a positive view of the human race is the best attitude to adopt. Of course, it must be coupled with common-sense precautions and the "existential alertness" that independent travelers often access. *Existential alertness* is a term that describes the state cultural strangers experience when they feel at risk in their new surroundings. In Myers-Briggs terms, this is a heightened use of the Sensing preference, and it makes travelers more alert and "switched on." It also helps them to more quickly find structure in the new culture and make sense of what is going on around them.

This positive attitude has, I believe, been largely responsible for eliciting a positive response from the people I have made contact with. I refuse to let unfounded anxieties prevent me from taking journeys or engaging in adventures that are more life enhancing than life threatening. Nor, on the same principle, should you condemn a whole nation because the actions of one of its nationals harm you.

The states that are driven by our external surroundings are the primary states. Then, as we reflect on the situations and work out what they mean to us, we move to the higher canopies of consciousness that Michael Hall refers to. So how, you may be asking, does one set about finding the higher "meta states" that are driving a particular state that is concerning us? You might use the following types of questions to establish what a particular issue really means to you. Any questions that ask what something means to you will tend to shift your thinking to a higher level of meaning. Choose an issue or problem and try answering some of the following questions (or similar types of questions that force you to reflect on the meaning of the issue). You may find that repeating certain questions leads you to yet higher levels. This process should lead you up through the layers or canopies of meaning until you reach the overarching meaning the issue or problem has for you. This meaning should represent the highest level, the level that governs all the ones below it.

- What is this issue about?
- How does this issue affect me?
- When I think about this issue, what do I feel?
- What is really important to me about this issue?
- What does that mean to me?
- Why is that important to me?
- What is important to me about that in particular?

You may need to ask fewer questions to reach the highest level, or you may need to ask more. The important thing is that you understand the principle of the procedure. Each time you ask yourself questions like "What does this mean to me?" or "Why is that important to me?" you move upward to the next level or canopy of meaning.

Sometimes just identifying the true reason for anxiety and being able to name or describe it is enough to collapse the chain. The highest canopy will always determine our response at lower levels. For example, most people would accept that the instinct to survive is hardwired into the human species. At the primary level, therefore, our actions would always support this instinct in a life-threatening situation. Yet people have laid down their lives for others throughout the history of humankind. Clearly, those who sacrificed themselves were responding to a state that supplanted their drive to survive. What overarching state could do that—a sense of duty or self-sacrifice, or a state of love? With this in mind, what higher state could you access that would override your unhelpful state? Try a state of resilience, a state of self-esteem, or even a state of inner peace and calm. You will know what the appropriate higher-level state is.

To make this clearer, I will give a personal example. In order to help overcome my fear of public speaking (a debilitating fear since I was embarking on a career as professional trainer), I changed my own perception of the role of a trainer. Previously I had seen the role of trainer as something akin to a presenter, and therefore my own role was as a professional presenter—literally a subject matter expert who should be able to answer any question directed at him. I thus put myself under tremendous pressure as I attempted to learn everything there was to know about every subject I had to present on, clearly an impossible task. How I used to dread the question that I knew must surely come, the one I would be completely unable to understand, let alone answer. However, once I changed my perception of the trainer's role from that of a presenter to that of a coach and facilitator, and changed my objective from wanting to impress to wanting to help, most of that self-imposed pressure melted away. This is change at a high meta level.

To illustrate how the process might assist in a cross-cultural context, let us cast one of our traveler caricatures, Please Like Me, as the character who finds himself in a negative state. Please Like Me is upset and depressed. Just four months into his first job abroad, and all homesickness and culture shock are well behind him. Please Like Me thought that he had fit in well and that he was liked by all his new work colleagues. That is, until he found out that the previous evening, they had all met after work for a social drink, and he had not been invited to join them. He is not only disappointed but also a little resentful. Were all their previous shows of friendship just a front? He recognizes that he is starting to make assumptions and climb the Ladder of Inference. Intellectually, he is aware that even four months in the culture, he is a relative newcomer, especially as the culture seems to be very group oriented, where friendships and trust are built up over long periods of time, and until he has done so, he will remain an outsider. However, blaming it on cultural differences does not make him feel any better.

As he reflected, he asked himself the following questions and generated the accompanying responses. The questions are worded slightly differently from the ones I gave as examples earlier, but the principle is still the same.

Question	Response
• What is upsetting me?	• The fact that they did not invite me.
• How is it affecting me?	• I'm feeling annoyed, resentful, low on energy, isolated.
• Why is it so important to me to be invited?	• I want to be seen as part of the group.
• Why is that so important to me?	• It's good to be liked by other people.
• What does it mean to me to be liked by other people?	• It shows that other people value me.

Question	*Response*
• Why is that important to me?	• It proves I am a worthwhile person.
• What does that mean to me?	• I want other people to make me feel worthwhile.
• And what does that mean?	• I need other people to feel worthwhile.
• And what does needing other people to feel worthwhile mean?	• It means that deep down I don't really think a lot of myself.

At this point Please Like Me may feel that his "navel gazing" session hasn't made him feel much better, and possibly even worse. However, he has started to realize that whatever the reason behind his work colleagues' failure to invite him along, they are not responsible for the way he currently feels about it and the negative impact it has had on him. Until he can separate these two strands—what actually happened and what he feels about what happened—it will be difficult for him to analyze cultural differences at anything more than a superficial and academic level. His own emotional response, driven by a poor self-concept, will always get in the way and influence his reading of any similar situation. This in fact relates to the defense mechanisms I referred to in Chapter 3 and the section on behavioral flexibility. What he needs, even more than the respect and esteem of his work colleagues, is to work on his own self-esteem.

Those who cross cultural borders and live abroad are challenged to examine not only the way they were brought up to view the world, but also how they view themselves. For some this may be an unsettling and disorientating experience, at least at first, but for others it may be a cathartic, exciting, and liberating experience. For all it is an opportunity for great personal learning and development that has the potential to change and broaden the way they view both the world and themselves, forever. This chapter has focused on equipping you with greater self-understanding and how to deal with the unhelpful responses that crossing cultures can elicit. The next chapter will focus on cultural differences and how they may impact you, the traveler.

PART II

Looking Out

CHAPTER
FIVE

Important Values Orientations for the Sojourner

So far I have concentrated on you, the culture crosser, and what personal skills, knowledge, and traits are likely to help you bridge cultures more successfully. Part II, "Looking Out," deals more with external knowledge that will help guide your thinking as you prepare for, and later reflect on, your cross-cultural experiences.

Frameworks to Explain Cultural Differences

There are numerous definitions of the word *culture*. In order to avoid confusion, I have adopted the following definition for the purposes of this book:

> Culture is the acquired learning of a group that gives its members a sense of who they are, of belonging, of how they should behave, and of what they should be doing; culture makes that group recognizably different from other groups.

Frameworks that describe dimensions of cultural difference can help you understand your own cultural programming and provide a structured approach by which to compare your cultural programming with that of your hosts. A number of frameworks exist and most of them overlap, at least to some extent. For those planning to travel in a different culture, what is important is not just knowing about and understanding cultural differences, whether in the form of a framework or not, but when and how to use that knowledge and when and how not to use it.

Cultural frameworks provide recognizable dimensions against which different cultures may be compared. More specifically, they provide a measure and an explanation of how different cultures prefer to approach and solve universal problems. I sometimes use the following hypothetical scenario to help describe some common dimensions of cultural difference. Remember that dimensions describe problems that apply to people from all cultures.

Imagine that a cruise liner develops rudder problems and is blown off course. All radio contact is lost and eventually the liner is shipwrecked on a reef. A group of passengers boards a life raft and lands on a desert island with, it seems, only a remote possibility of rescue. However, they are not alone; about sixty other survivors comprising a mixture of male and female, old and young, all in various states of health and fitness, also manage to escape from the sinking liner and land on the island. Together they must face common issues of survival. What kind of society should they create?

Suppose only five of the survivors have the skill and agility to climb the palms and knock down the green coconuts; should they do this for the benefit of the whole group or just for themselves? In fact, do the survivors perceive themselves as one group, a bunch of disparate individuals, or a set of smaller and discrete groups with their own affiliations and loyalties?

Let's say the majority view is that they are all in it together and should stick together and work as a group. How would the group maintain cohesion? What behaviors would encourage group cohesion and what behaviors would tend to split the group up?

With limited resources to allocate, the group will have to make some important decisions. How will these be made, and who will make them? What kind of leader will the group most readily accept? Will the preference be for an older, wiser person or someone who can demonstrate the qualities of a leader, regardless of age?

It cannot be long before the precariousness of their position sinks in, if it did not at the start. Will they be rescued and survive? Stress levels are high as they think the unthinkable. How do the members of the group deal with the uncertainty; what coping mechanisms do they employ? Do they find some comfort in establishing routines and formulating rules to control the group's behavior, thus giving them the illusion that they are in control? As the thinking and logic behind some of the routines become lost or irrelevant, are these routines continued as rituals? Maybe religion provides some solace, or maybe some of the group feel that their fate is really out of their hands and that destiny will decide the eventual outcome. Conversely, maybe the uncertainty of when, or indeed whether, they will be rescued is a reality that the group can deal with and accept, even if they do not particularly like it.

It is a fact of life that people are born with different gifts, both physical and intellectual. What are the group's priorities? In what direction do group members channel their energy? Do they work toward accumulating surplus resources, toward escape, or simply toward making their current situation more comfortable? Also, how does the group deal with those members who are less well equipped to cope or contribute, who cannot pull their weight? Are they cared for as a matter of course, or are their failings a contentious issue?

Finally, what is the status of women versus men? Are the sexes considered equals, or is one higher in status? Is one sex expected to take on certain tasks based on gender? Whose opinion is the more influential? I will refer back to this scenario later in the chapter when we look at dimensions of cultural difference one by one. First, though, let's look at how cultural frameworks can be useful.

When Cultural Frameworks Are Useful

BEFORE A CULTURAL ENCOUNTER TAKES PLACE. Frameworks can help facilitate your own planning and expectations so that you are not entering a situation cold, with no information at all. Some preparation may be necessary before the encounter. For example: What behavior will be most helpful in building rapport with the hosts? Are differences in cultural values likely to raise any issues around status, class, gender, or ethnicity? What else do you need to be aware of? Of course, there are also practical and logistical issues, such as selecting the most appropriate clothing to wear. For example, if you are a Western woman traveling to a Muslim culture, you will need to decide if your opinion of what is appropriate dress is going to be in line with the local standards at your destination. Or if you are a businessman traveling to negotiate a foreign contract, what level of formality do you need to adopt, not only to show respect to your hosts but also to ensure that they take you seriously and accord you the same respect?

AFTER A CULTURAL ENCOUNTER. For cultural learning to occur, you have to reflect on your experiences and then put them into some sort of contextual framework that enables you to understand what you have experienced. In cultures noticeably different from your own, this can be almost impossible to do if you have had only limited exposure to the culture. In fact, it sometimes remains a challenge even for those who have spent a number of years in a culture. Having some knowledge of the key areas in which cultures differ in terms of values and basic assumptions greatly facilitates this reflective phase of the experiential learning cycle.

When Not to Use Cultural Frameworks

Using frameworks of cultural differences is counterproductive when you are actually interacting with someone. It is very easy to begin relating the behavior you are witnessing directly to some cultural dimension and then jump to a judgment based on the strength of—what? Not much evidence at all usually. I have been guilty of this myself on occasion, and from chastening experience I now believe that it is far more important and effective to focus your attention on whoever is in front of you and on what she is saying. Your listening should be empathetic. You should be totally in the moment, and to do this your mind must be as clear and open as possible, not striving to make judgments and comparisons but to understand the other's perspective. It is also more respectful to your hosts to pay them the courtesy of your full attention. You otherwise run the real risk of sounding like someone interviewing job candidates who has already made up her mind about an applicant in the first few seconds of the interview, but who then goes on to pigeonhole the unfortunate individual. The rest of the interview then consists merely of selectively seeking evidence to support and justify her decision while ignoring all evidence to the contrary.

In addition to possibly jumping to the wrong conclusions, you may miss valuable clues in what the person right in front of you is saying, both verbally and nonverbally, simply because your attention is split, and therefore diluted as you mentally try to match what you are seeing and hearing against a cultural dimension.

Last but by no means least, always think of the impression your behavior may have on your host. Most people know when the person they are speaking to is not really listening or paying full attention to them. This is the case even when speaking over a phone line. If you give others the impression that your mind is half elsewhere, what will their interpretation be? Put yourself in their shoes and think how you would interpret the situation.

How Not to Use Cultural Frameworks

Cross-cultural frameworks and models should not be used as reliable pre-dictors of individual behavior. Nor should they be seen as a panacea for dealing with all cultural differences or as a set of mechanical instructions that will open all doors into a new culture:

- You should always stand as close as . . .
- You must always take into account that . . .
- Always respond in this specific way when they . . .
- The correct communication style to adopt in this culture is . . .

And so on. Admittedly, sometimes such direction proves to be uncannily ac-curate. Nevertheless, that is no excuse for not using your own eyes, ears, and head to assess the situation and then make your own first-hand-assessment. Also, cultures do change, albeit slowly, so models based on observations or test scores made in the past will gradually become dated. South Korea, for example, illustrates this point quite well. L. Robert Kohls, in his book *Learn-ing to Think Korean* (2001), describes how the people of North and South Korea have probably seen more change in the space of five years than many countries see in twenty-five. Kohls also describes how cultural values within South Korea have shifted to meet the country's changing circumstances, so much so that the values held by South Korean people may vary depending on the decade in which they were born. Most cultures undergo changes in values, but the degree of shift will obviously vary according to the circum-stances of each culture.

Another accusation often leveled at frameworks of national culture is that they reinforce and promote national stereotyping. The frameworks represent cultural norms that reflect the viewpoint of the majority of each sample. In effect, they are broad generalizations that ignore the individuals who fall out-side local social norms. Therefore, it is important to use frameworks with this in mind and to remember the caveat provided in the previous section that when you are actually communicating with someone from another culture, your attention should be on that person rather than mentally referring to a cultural framework. Finally, another problematic issue is how people choose to use frameworks. Just as statistics can be manipulated to provide supporting evidence or to add spurious scientific weight to almost any claim, frameworks of cultural difference, if used as a definitive bellwether of any culture (which they most certainly are not), may be open to similar abuse.

How Best to Use Cultural Frameworks

Frameworks (or any models) are best seen as a sort of compass bearing rather than as a detailed map. They can provide the user with a sense of direction but do not show all the variation of terrain that a detailed topographical map would provide. As such, frameworks simply provide the sojourner with more information on which to form a best first guess and from which he may be able to roughly predict some of the patterns of behavior he is likely to encounter.

What Are Cultural Frameworks?

Most, if not all, frameworks arise out of a study of a sample taken from a population segment of a culture, which is then compared against samples from other cultures. For a framework to measure differences between one culture and another successfully, the dimensions selected must apply equally to all human beings. These dimensions may best be described as universal problems that all humans have to solve. How they are solved by different cultures will vary for a variety of reasons, including climate, geography, natural resources, historical events such as invasion and occupations, availability of food, and so on. Comparisons between the cultural samples are made on the basis of how the majority of the sample population responds to the questionnaires, value orientation studies, surveys, case studies, or whatever methodology the researchers employ to garner their information.

The results or scores are usually averaged to reflect the majority opinion of each culture sample. In other words, the results will not represent individuals whose choices differ significantly from those of their fellow citizens. Nevertheless, cultural frameworks are likely to be fairly accurate as predictors of how social organizations and systems will be structured and practiced within different cultures. This is because systems, in order to work, tend to reflect and be shaped by the values of the majority rather than those exceptional individuals who fall outside the normal distribution.

What Behavior Do Frameworks Measure?

As a society develops and becomes more structured, social rules are developed that define what constitutes acceptable and unacceptable, even taboo, behavior. Those who violate these rules incur some penalty or punishment. Children raised within the society soon learn to conform to the behavior they see around them every day and which is reinforced by teachers and parents. In this respect, cultural programming is not so much learned as acquired.

So how much of an influence does culture have on our behavior? To answer this question and at the same time put it into context, we first need to identify what the ranges of potential influence are. Broadly speaking, there are three sources or levels of influence on human behavior:

1. The universal level
2. The collective level
3. The individual level

THE UNIVERSAL LEVEL. All, or nearly all, of the human race shares this level of influence. It has been referred to as the biological "operating system" of humans. Behavior such as crying, laughing, the need to connect with other people, reciprocation of kindness, and the drive to find a mate and to reproduce are all part of this level, which is part of our genetic inheritance as humans.

THE COLLECTIVE LEVEL. This is the level that cultural frameworks and dimensions of cultural difference address. Behavior at this level is specific to certain groups or categories; it is behavior you acquire from the society you are brought up in. The whole area of subjective culture falls under this category; for example, what behavior is considered normal or abnormal, how people usually expect to be greeted or to greet others; what managerial behavior is considered acceptable or unacceptable, how men relate to women and vice versa, and how older generations view the younger. Also falling within this level are prescribed behaviors for basic functions such as eating and drinking and for the collective rituals that surround death and burial. The pattern and style of communication usually adopted in various situations also form part of this level, as does knowing the correct distance to stand from the person you are communicating with. This brief list does not even touch the surface of what could have been included, but hopefully it has given you some idea of the scope of culture's influence on our behavior.

The collective level of influence governs our values at a deep level, with regard to a vast range of human activity and thinking. Probably the best-known and certainly the most-cited living author in the field of cross-cultural research is Geert Hofstede (2001, 9). His definition of culture describes this level: "the collective programming of the mind which distinguishes the members of one group or category of people from another." The group or category in this case is the national group, although the same definition could just as easily describe a professional group such as doctors, accountants, engineers, politicians, and so forth. Often we are unaware of how our cultural programming influences us daily in our decisions of what is good or bad, ethical or unethical, appropriate or inappropriate, clean or dirty, beautiful or ugly, just or unjust, and so on. Usually it is only when people step outside their own culture into a completely different one that they question the source and validity of their own value judgments. And there are probably many who travel to different cultures without ever wondering at the differences they see all around them.

THE INDIVIDUAL LEVEL. This level of behavior is unique to each individual. It is formed from the combination of the genes we inherit from our parents, which help determine physical characteristics and temperament, and is shaped and influenced by our own unique personality, talents, and life experiences. This is the level that the Myers-Briggs Type Indicator examines.

Frameworks attempt to describe and explain differences in national values within the collective level. However, it is clear that all the levels overlap, and in reality there is no consensus on what defines the boundary between one level and another. We cannot distinguish what percentages of a person's actions are driven by his or her individual personality, by cultural upbringing, or by some primordial universal instinct.

Cultural Dimensions in Action

Let us now look at dimensions of cultural difference and some of the issues facing our hapless maroons.

Individualism versus Collectivism

First, a group of over sixty people is a big group to have on an island, which by definition has limited resources. The survivors themselves have different survival capabilities. Some may actually feel that they would be better on their own, unencumbered by any concerns for the rest of the group. To what extent, then, should the group remain together? Should it be one cohesive unit, several smaller groups, or a loose collection of disparate individuals? The problem of establishing what control, if any, the group should have over the individual has faced all societies at some stage in their various developments. In the anthropological and intercultural field, this dilemma is usually referred to as the *individualism/collectivism dichotomy*. The terms have no political connotation. (I will include and explain other recognized terms in my descriptions throughout this book so that readers who are new to this area of study will find other intercultural literature, which refers to the same dimensions, more accessible.)

Collectivism in this sense refers to the extent to which individuals feel controlled by the collective will of the society in which they live and were raised. Take, for example, the problem of water supply for the irrigation of terraced rice paddy fields on the hill slopes of places like Bali in Indonesia and Banaue on the island of Luzon in the northern Philippines. The terraces on Banaue were created by the Ifugao farmers more than two thousand years ago and are now listed by UNESCO as a world heritage site. The terraces are shelved on an incline of one thousand meters and cover a land base of four hundred kilometers. The terraces themselves are walled with river stones wherever the earth is of such an unstable character that it needs walls. Some of the terrace walls rise as high as twenty feet. The paddy fields are irrigated by an amazing system of bamboo pipes that carry the mountain stream water to the terraces and then from higher to lower terraces by gravity.

It is obvious that the initial construction and maintenance and the continuing operation of the terraces require community effort. The water supply to farmers lower down on the slope depends largely on how much those higher up and nearer to the source of the spring allow to flow to them. The lower farmers are also at the mercy of the farmers higher up for the direction of the water flow—whether it is away from or toward them. The only way that an agrarian society such as this can function is through close, and at times complex, cooperation and a system of controls that ensures collective obedience to the community rules. In these circumstances "doing your own thing" without regard for others would probably result in some collective censure of the individual's actions and possible marginalization or rejection from the group itself.

In contrast, *individualism* is when an individual has learned to act independently from other members of the group or society to which he or she belongs. The United States is an example of a highly individualistic culture. People refer to the frontier spirit that helped shape the country into what it is today, and there can be no doubt that being independent minded and having the ability to stand up for oneself meant that more opportunities were available in those early frontier days. However, even within individualistic cultures, some communities are clearly more collectivistic than others.

Usually, smaller towns that are focused around one main industry, such as fishing, mining, or agriculture, tend more toward the collectivist rather than the individualist end of the scale.

This dimension, therefore, presents a continuum. At the individualistic end of the scale are cultures where the interests of the individual prevail over the interests of the group. In collectivist cultures there is a tendency for the task to take precedence over individual preferences. Look for clues that indicate a broad preference for one over the other. For example, the existence of large extended families tends to inculcate a group-oriented outlook. How people describe themselves in conversation—for example, frequent use of the collective "we" as opposed to "I"—can also provide telling indicators. Notice also how considerate people seem to be of others' needs when working or socializing. Being "other-directed" is not the sole preserve of group-oriented cultures, but it is clearly more of a prerequisite for social acceptance in those societies than it is in individualistic cultures. If you visit a country during the holiday season, notice whether vacationers seem to include whole families, including grandparents and other relatives, or consist of parents and their children only, couples, or even solo travelers.

The following list highlights some of the key differences between collectivistic and individualistic cultures. It describes the more extreme characteristics that you could expect to see at each end of the continuum. Most cultures have elements of both, so you will have to use your judgment to work out where the balance lies.

Compare the two columns and determine which side describes your own culture most closely. Next, look down the list again and identify which side, on balance, actually appeals to you the most. As we go through the other dimensions, you should be able to build a profile of your own culture as well as the cultural values with which you feel most comfortable.

Collectivistic
- People tend to identify with the group they are in. For example, "I'm a miner" or "I work for Acme Inc."
- People belong to extended families and clans who offer protection in return for their loyalty.

Individualistic
- People clearly see themselves as an individual entity. "Hi, my name's Alan."

- Individuals are brought up to look after themselves and their immediate family.

Collectivistic

- Work and social life are intertwined.
- Failure results in a sense of shame that you have let down others who were depending on you. As a result, you lose face.
- Employees of organizations see themselves as members of an ingroup with moral obligations to that group.
- A lot of time, effort, and expense is devoted to building and maintaining social and business relationships.

Individualistic

- Personal privacy is valued and protected.
- Failure results in a sense of guilt that you have not given a good enough account of yourself and that you have not lived up to your own self-image.
- Employees are joined to organizations by a contract, and their involvement in the organization is more contractual than moral.
- Often the task takes precedence over the relationship if there is a conflict of interest between the two.

In Geert Hofstede's 1980 landmark cultural survey, the United States had the highest score at the individualistic end of the continuum, with Australia, Canada, and Britain close behind. Venezuela scored as the most collectivistic, and Columbia and Pakistan were not far behind. With a few exceptions, there seems to be an East-West split, with Eastern countries being more group oriented or collectivistic and Western countries more individualistic.

It is important for you, the sojourner, to be able to recognize the characteristics of each dimension so you can determine which dimension predominates in a given community. This means much more than simply remembering what score a country got in a survey administered many years ago. Take your cues from those you meet and converse with. Are they brisk and businesslike, or do they take their time getting to know you? In collectivistic cultures, those who first approach you informally and go out of their way to make contact shortly after your arrival may not be typical of the local population. Beware of making false assumptions about the culture as a whole based on the behavior of one or two individuals. Those from individualistic cultures entering collectivist cultures are often told to "build the relationship" without being told what this means. Though wining and dining may be a part of relationship building, more important by far are qualities such as honesty, sincerity, reliability, dependability, mutual trust, competence, and a focus on the other person's needs and well-being.

Let's return to the island scenario and consider another cultural dimension.

Power Distance

We have already noted that our desert island has limited resources. How will they be apportioned or allocated? This question flags another issue that humans around the world have had to solve. This dimension is about influence and power and is usually referred to as *power distance*.

More specifically, this dimension is about how power is acquired and used. In some cultures there seems to be a continual striving by those on the lower rungs of the social ladder to narrow the gap, catch up, and maybe even overtake those who are considered to be on higher rungs. At the same time, an equal effort is being made by those already highly positioned to maintain and even increase their distance from those below. An alternative to this state of affairs is where people at each level still try to better their lot but at the same time accept a basic assumption that people are not equal and that the stability of society is largely dependent on a communal acceptance of this fact.

In some cultures there is an acceptance, even an expectation, that there will be inequalities in how power is distributed. These cultures are described as having a high power distance. In such cultures, inequalities between people are expected and seen as desirable. The difference between those holding power and those having little or none at all is obvious and indeed emphasized.

Here is a personal example. I was once training a team of British scientific and technical staff led by a senior manager. The senior manager, apart from being very knowledgeable and experienced, was self-effacing and modest. His management style was relaxed, consensual, and egalitarian. As a result, he was very popular in the comparatively low power distance culture of both Britain and the organization in which he worked. Unfortunately, he maintained the same approach when VIP customers from South Korea and Japan were visiting his site for the first time. In his typical fashion, he met the arriving car himself, opened the car door, and helped the visitors through the building, opening more doors along the way until they finally reached his office on the second floor. When the office door was opened for them, they expected to see the senior manager sitting impressively at his desk. Instead it finally dawned on them that the helpful and seemingly obsequious man who had led them through the building and whom they had taken for a junior clerk (and may have inadvertently treated as such, perhaps even letting him carry their bags) was in fact the senior man they had come to see!

In a low-power-distance culture his actions would probably be seen as a laudable display of personal customer care. To the high-power-distance visitors, however, his actions cast him in a different light. What sort of senior manager has no staff to carry out his menial duties? Was he really a senior manager? Also, his demeanor and the way he rushed up to the car on their arrival had given them no indication of his true status; he had effectively lured them into a potentially embarrassing situation right from the start. In acting like a lackey and bag carrier, he had unwittingly tempted the visitors to use him as one. In the cultures the visitors had come from, they were used to being able to quickly establish somebody's status in relation to their own and thus be able to show the correct level of politeness and respect. The Brit's amiable low-power-distance approach, far from making his visitors feel at ease, had actually led them to feel confused and uneasy.

In a country scoring low on this dimension, inequalities among people tend to be minimized; people are generally encouraged to treat others as equals and work toward a "level playing field"—at least officially. The Brit in the example is clearly comfortable in a low-power-distance culture and might find it difficult to adapt his management style to suit a high-power-distance culture. In that business environment, he would probably feel stifled by his own manager, who would seem autocratic and directive. Moreover, his own staff would likely be frustrated by his "soft" consensual approach. The Brit's attempts to involve his staff by asking for their opinion on how a particular job should be done would probably be received in silence. They would be reluctant to put forward an idea that, first, might result in a loss of face if it were not accepted, or second, that might embarrass the British boss if their idea were clearly better than his. And third, how can they tell a boss directly that it is his job to manage, it's what he gets paid for, and why should his staff do his job for him?

The best way to measure power distance in a culture is by surveying the views of the less powerful members—those on the lower rungs of the social ladder and in lower levels within institutions and organizations—to see if they accept that power should be distributed unequally. Canvasing the views of the higher echelons would probably not be so effective, because in most cultures those at the top would agree that they have every right to be there because they are special in some way. At the lower end of the social scale, however, there is far more cultural variation on this issue.

Countries that are considered to be high-power-distance cultures include Malaysia, Panama, the Philippines, Indonesia, and Venezuela. Also high on this dimension are those Eastern countries that were influenced by Confucian philosophy, such as China, Korea, Japan, Singapore, and Taiwan. One of the tenets of Confucian teaching is the ordering and observation of relationships by status. High-power-distance cultures often score high on the collectivistic scale as well.

Austria, Israel, Denmark, New Zealand, Norway, and Sweden scored equally low on the power distance dimension; Britain, the United States, Australia, Switzerland, and Germany were close behind. France, however, scored as a high-power-distance culture, ranking approximately fifteenth from the top in the Hofstede survey.

Once again, let us look at some of the key differences that may exist at each end of this continuum. As with the previous dimension, look down the two lists and decide which column describes your own culture most closely and then identify which side, on balance, actually appeals to you the most.

High Power Distance	*Low Power Distance*
• Inequalities between people are expected and desired.	• Inequalities between people should be minimized.
• We should show due respect to those of higher status.	• We should treat each other as equals.
• Dependency needs must be met. Those higher placed have an obligation to look after those in their charge, who in turn should respond with loyalty and respect.	• Harmony exists between the powerful and the powerless if each accepts the skills and worth of the other.
• Those in positions of authority tend to be inaccessible and do not play down their position or power.	• Those in power tend to publicly downplay their authority and often boast that their office door is always open.
• Power, position, and status can be ascribed or given. Respect comes with the title.	• Power, position, and status should ideally be earned through ability and won on merit.
• Hierarchical and pyramidal organizational structures are acceptable and normal.	• Flatter organizational structures are seen as more progressive.

High Power Distance	Low Power Distance
• Age, wisdom, and life's experience are valued for their own sake.	• Ability and qualifications to fulfill the role are valued.

If you plan to visit or even live in a new country, polite, respectful behavior will generally serve you well in both low- and high-power-distance cultures as will the "conscious humility"—a realistic appreciation of self—mentioned in Chapter 1. Once you have established, through your observations and discussions with colleagues and local contacts, which end of the continuum best represents the host culture, you can begin to adapt your behavior more specifically.

The Need for Structure

Although uncertainty is a subjective experience (that is, some people feel more comfortable in unpredictable situations than others), feelings of uncertainty may also be shared to some extent through cultural heritage. Take, for example, the uncertainty caused by the possibility of invasion that has historically faced smaller countries, such as South Korea, that are bounded by larger and more powerful neighbors. In other countries, such as Japan, features of the land itself—earthquakes, active volcanoes, severe storms, and a chronic shortage of natural resources such as oil, iron, copper, and arable land—may cause uncertainty. Other countries have a history of vulnerability. Germany, for instance, bounded by nine other countries, has experienced almost constant redefinition of its borders over the last hundred years.

Cultures develop collective patterns of behavior to cope with the stress and uncertainty these threats cause. Usually these responses are inculcated into the population at a young age through education by the family, schools, and the state. In Japan, for example, people are brought up to be conscious about the need to conserve resources and to recycle waste whenever possible. This dimension, then, is about the degree to which people within a culture prefer structured or unstructured situations—situations where the outcome is predictable or situations that are novel and unpredictable.

Unpredictable and ambiguous situations can be a source of stress. Take an everyday event such as a business meeting between two people or two groups. Let's assume they are all meeting for the first time. In some cultures the unpredictability of not knowing the people and how they will respond is not an issue that requires extensive thought, planning, or structure because once the meeting is underway, relevant information about the other members will emerge in the normal course of events. In some cultures, however, unpredictability is an issue, and one that causes high levels of apprehension. As a result, strategies have been adopted collectively that make such first-time encounters more structured and predictable. In countries such as Japan and Korea, the exchange of business cards provides a standard ritual whereby all the essential information needed to enable them communicate correctly with the other person, such as rank, status, and size of organization, is quickly obtained at the start.

Although this dimension is usually referred to as *uncertainty avoidance,* in simple terms it is the attempt to reduce the negative impact of uncertainty. A common response to an uncertain situation is to try to impose some sort of order and structure. This may or may not change the situation overall, but it can make the circumstances seem less stressful.

Anyone who has ever traveled in Japan has enjoyed some of the benefits of a highly structured society. Trains leave the station consistently at the scheduled time and public facilities are maintained to a high standard across the country. An excellent public transport system, however, cannot prevent the foreign visitor from finding himself lost, as I was on several occasions. When I asked directions from local Japanese, they usually drew a map for me that showed in precise terms how to get from where I was to where I wanted to go. These maps invariably provided accurate directions and a large amount of detail that I am sure would have been left out if I had I asked for a similar map back home. The directions were completely unambiguous and the maps showed each small alleyway. It was as if people were afraid to leave anything to chance. Other travelers I spoke to commented that they had experienced the same precision.

Thus, what is measured by this dimension is the degree to which people in a country prefer structure. Are they generally flexible and easygoing, or is daily life filled with formality, rules, and particular ways of doing things that people tend to follow? Countries that scored high in uncertainty avoidance are those cultures that find the uncertainties of life threatening. They strive to control them. In such cultures, structure and formality are a means to provide consistency, predictability, and control, even if the control is largely illusory. What is different is often seen as dangerous as well, and those who deviate from normal social behavior find society intolerant and often hostile.

Countries that scored low on this dimension are described as having low uncertainty avoidance. This is characterized by a greater acceptance that uncertainty is a fact of life. What is different is more likely to be seen as interesting rather than threatening.

This is not an easy dimension to understand. If you are still struggling, think in terms of structure, formality, rules, and set procedures versus relaxed, flexible, and easygoing patterns of behavior. The following list of some of the key differences should help to make the distinction clearer.

High Uncertainty Avoidance
- More rules and a greater degree of structure are desirable.
- There tends to be more ritual behavior.
- Time is valuable and should be controlled. Things tend to run on time.

- There is an inner urge to work hard. Activity reduces stress.
- Set routines exist to standardize procedures and make situations more predictable.

- There is a high regard for knowledge and experts.

Low Uncertainty Avoidance
- Fewer written rules and less structure are preferred.
- There tends to be less ritual behavior.
- Time is free and is simply a means by which to orient yourself. Timetables and schedules are, in reality, unreliable guides.
- Hard work in itself is not seen as virtuous.
- Informality and spontaneity lead to different ways of handling the same procedures.
- There is a high regard for practical common sense and general knowledge.

As with the previous two dimensions, decide which list describes your own culture most closely and then identify which side, on balance, appeals to you the most.

Countries that scored high on uncertainty avoidance include Greece, Germany, Uruguay, Portugal, Japan, and Brazil. Cultures scoring a tolerance for uncertainty (that is, low on this continuum) are Ireland, Denmark, Sweden, Great Britain, Hong Kong, and New Zealand.

How this dimension will affect you as a sojourner depends on the difference between your own culture and the one you are visiting and, of course, on your temperament. The new culture may be the complete opposite of what you are used to, but it may actually appeal to you more. However, if this is not the case, then you will need to draw on those important cross-cultural traits covered in Chapter 3, particularly in the section on behavioral flexibility. For example, you may have to remind yourself to stay relaxed when things do not always run on schedule, not to get annoyed if the level of formality seems excessive, and so on. Try to work out the logic or thinking behind why things are done the way they are.

Let us go back to our island scenario for a final time.

The Drive to Achieve

We have already noted the variation that exists within the group of castaways. Certain tasks will be beyond the capability of some of the group, and physical frailty may rule out some members from activity altogether. Because resources are limited, decisions must be made on how to apportion them. What qualities will prove most useful to the group in this situation? On the one hand, there are those who are able to take some risks in order to obtain more food and resources; they are even prepared to go beyond what is immediately required so as to build up the existing stores to ensure adequate supplies against the unexpected. On the other hand, some people may feel that it is more important to focus on the wider needs of the group once the survival needs have been met. What about the quality of life on the island, and what provision should be made to care for the old, the weak, and others incapable of looking after themselves?

This dimension looks at how societies balance the need to achieve against quality of life. If a society is achievement oriented, then values such as assertiveness, competition, and high performance will be held in high regard. In a society more oriented toward quality of life, values such as community service, solidarity, and personal relationships are highly regarded. For example, is it considered more important to strive to win, to achieve, and to progress than it is to ensure a higher quality of life for everyone, including those members of society less able to look after themselves? In a way, this dimension is about quality versus quantity, about whether we live to work or work to live. If you plan to read other books on cultural frameworks, it is worth noting that the achievement-oriented cultures are sometimes described as *masculine* cultures, and those cultures oriented more toward quality of life are described as *feminine* cultures.

In his book *The Mind of the Strategist* (1982), Kenichi Ohmae recalls his own experience from the ages of six to twelve in primary school in Japan and how the precarious nature of Japan's survival was drilled into him. "No resources and over one hundred million people to feed," he and all the other young pupils were repeatedly reminded. The only solution, the school children were told, was for Japan to import raw materials, add value to them, and then export finished goods for a profit, from which food could be purchased. Ohmae suggests that this cultural upbringing is the mainspring of the workaholic nature of the Japanese. People were afraid *not* to work hard.

The following list gives some of the key differences for this dimension.

Achievement
- People live to work: Achievement is most important.
- Decisiveness is admired.
- Ambition motivates people to work hard.
- Money and material things are important.
- Success and achievement are admired and rewarded.
- Job stress is prevalent.
- Fewer women have high-ranking, well-paid jobs.
- Control and power are used to achieve goals.

Quality of Life
- People work to live: Quality of life is most important.
- Problem solving invariably takes people into account.
- The desire to provide service is a motivating factor.
- People and the quality of life are important.
- Sympathy is with the underdog.
- High job stress is less prevalent.
- More women are qualified and have high-ranking, well-paid jobs.
- Persuasion and consensus are used to achieve goals.

As with the previous three dimensions, identify which side describes your own culture most accurately and which appeals to you the most.

The country that ranked the highest toward achievement was in fact Japan, followed by Austria, Venezuela, Italy, and Mexico. At the quality of life end of the continuum were Sweden, Norway, the Netherlands, Denmark, Costa Rica, France, and Iran.

It is common for people to have a strong personal affinity for one end of the continuum over the other. As a result, travelers may seek common ground with local contacts by assuming they share the same preference. For example, an achievement-oriented sojourner posted to Austria, a country that scored strongly toward achievement, may assume that any Austrian she speaks to shares similar values in this regard. This is not necessarily the case. Just because someone conforms to how society expects her to behave does not mean she would not prefer to behave in a different way if she could do so without censure. As mentioned earlier, it is unwise to make assumptions about an individual based purely on a cultural framework. Also, if a local who prefers quality of life over achievement still conforms to fit into his own culture, then the sojourner will be expected to adapt some of his behavior to fit in as well. For example, if you work in an office in Japan and always leave work well before all your Japanese work colleagues, then you are effectively signaling that you do not want to conform to what is considered normal behavior in Japan. As a result, you may find it more difficult to be accepted by your colleagues.

So far I have introduced four dimensions and shown how human values can vary in relation to them.

- The control of the group over individuals—individualism versus collectivism
- How power is acquired and used—power distance
- The need for structure—uncertainty avoidance
- The drive to achieve versus quality of life—masculine or feminine culture

However, these are by no means the only dimensions that have been identified. Following are some other dimensions, the characteristics of which you may recognize if you have interacted with people from a range of different cultures.

Universalism versus Particularism

The universalism/particularism dimension is often linked to the individualism/collectivism dimension, mainly because those in individualistic cultures are more likely to want to apply a universal ruling (that is, a ruling that will apply equally to everyone). Those coming from a collectivistic culture, on the other hand, see more logic in applying different sets of rules to different people depending on whether they are members of a particular group or not—a particularist approach. The insiders invariably get a better deal than the outsiders.

An interesting way of explaining this dimension is to use the approach employed by Fons Trompenaars to highlight and measure cultural differences. Trompenaars and Charles Hampden-Turner (1997) posed human dilemmas of the type that typically occur in cross-cultural encounters. These dilemmas were presented to survey participants, who then had to choose from a range of possible responses. One of his best-known scenarios is that of the car and the pedestrian, originally written by two Americans, Samuel A. Stouffer and Jackson Toby (1951). The following is quoted directly from the second edition of Trompenaars and Hampden-Turner's book *Riding the Waves of Culture* (1997, 33–34).

> You are riding in a car driven by a close friend. He hits a pedestrian. You know he was going at least 35 miles per hour in an area of the city where the maximum allowed speed is 20 miles per hour. There are no witnesses. His lawyer says that if you testify under oath that he was driving only 20 miles per hour, it may save him from serious consequences.
>
> What right has your friend to expect you to protect him?
>
> **1.** My friend has a definite right as a friend to expect me to testify to the lower figure.
> **2.** He has some right as a friend to expect me to testify to the lower figure.
> **3.** He has no right as a friend to expect me to testify to the lower figure.
>
> What do you think you would do in view of the obligations of a sworn witness and the obligation to your friend?
>
> **1.** Testify that he was going 20 miles an hour.
> **2.** Not testify that he was going 20 miles an hour.

The dimension of universalism and particularism is about rules versus relationships. Universalistic cultures show a broad preference for general rules and codes of practice that are applied equally to everyone in society. The rule of law, for example, should take precedence over the needs of colleagues, friends, and relations. The dilemma about the car and the pedestrian is based around this dimension. Few people from a universalistic culture thought that their friend had any right to expect them to testify that they were driving at a lower speed than was actually the case.

In a particularistic culture, the response to such a question would depend on the particular situation. In the case of this dilemma, a close friend is an important relationship, and so more respondents in the particularistic culture felt that their friend had some right to expect their assistance.

Participants from universalistic cultures, on the other hand, although also feeling sympathy for the friend, were more likely to feel that the friend did not have a right to expect their support in such a situation. Trompenaars also discovered that for some participants, the more serious the accident— for example, if the pedestrian had been killed—the less they were inclined to support their friend; it was serious so the law would have to decide the outcome. For others, the opposite was true; their friend was clearly in greater need of their help if the pedestrian died as a result of the accident. If they had been undecided as to the rights of their friend when first told of the dilemma, then the further news that the pedestrian had died made it clear that the consequences for their friend were also more serious, and so the decision was easier—they must support their friend.

Clearly, both sides can make a strong moral defense for their point of view, and you no doubt have your own opinion about what is right or wrong. The key is to be able to feel something of what those at the other end of the scale are feeling and to understand the logic of their viewpoint.

The car and the pedestrian is a dilemma that people around the world find difficult to resolve. On the one hand, everyone feels something for the law, justice, the pedestrian, and his family and relatives. People also feel loyalty to their friends and a desire to protect them. Trompenaars suggests that to understand another cultural viewpoint, you must first find the other point of view within yourself. In this case, for example, if you feel that the law should be upheld and that your friend has no right to expect you to give false evidence, then replace the friend in the dilemma with a member of your own family. Does your universal viewpoint change to a particularistic one if the person in court is your wife, husband, son, daughter, mother, or father? Adding this further restriction to the scenario gives the universalist an opportunity to experience the particularist point of view.

As with the previous dimensions, compare the following lists and decide which one describes your own culture most accurately and which is most appealing.

Universalist	*Particularist*
• Rules should apply equally to all.	• How rules are applied depends on the situation and on who is involved.
• Once a contract has been finalized, those involved should stand by what has been agreed.	• Contracts should be modifiable to accommodate changing circumstances.
• There is only one truth and it applies to everyone.	• There can be many different versions of the truth, each valid depending on your point of view.
• Rules are more important than relationships.	• Relationships come before rules.
• "Insider" and "outsider" distinctions are seen as unfair.	• "Insider" and "outsider" distinctions are seen as normal.

Countries that scored toward the particularistic end of the continuum include South Korea, Venezuela, Russia, China, India, Bulgaria, Indonesia, and Greece. Countries that scored higher on the universalistic end of the continuum include Switzerland, the United States, Canada, Sweden, Australia, the United Kingdom, the Netherlands, and Germany.

When you enter a new culture, the level of adjustment you need to make will depend on the type of culture you come from and the type of culture you are visiting. Until you have established what the difference is, it is probably a safe strategy to note and initially follow the "what not to dos" of both ends of the continuum. Hopefully this will help you avoid getting off on the wrong foot before you even settle in.

For example, do not take small talk lightly and certainly do not dismiss it as a waste of time. If someone challenges you with a rational, logical argument, do not assume that they do not like or respect you as a person. Do not take it as a personal insult if you are asked to prove yourself despite your proven connections. Do not underestimate the value and effectiveness of personal networks. Do not dismiss a talented individual who is not connected. Do not make a decision based on an assumption that you are part of an ingroup; make sure that you are part of it first. Do not automatically expect to be made a special case because of who you are and who you know.

Neutral versus Emotional

This dimension is really about how emotions are expressed. In cultures that can be considered neutral, the open display of emotion is neither expected nor encouraged. Appearing cool, detached, and in control of your emotions will win you respect. Conversely, in cultures that are considered emotional, it is acceptable, even expected, that you will display your feelings. In emotional cultures, when appropriate, your public behavior may include the full gamut of emotions from loud, excitable, and bellicose anger to open sorrow and grief or simple disappointment. In emotional cultures the standard physical distance between two people conversing is often closer than in neutral cultures, and there may be more actual physical contact.

When you arrive in another culture, listen for how willingly and openly people express what and how they are feeling. Do they openly express their emotions? Do they talk about their feelings at all? How do the locals generally interact with each other? Look and listen for high-energy, animated conversations where the listener may start to respond before the speaker has finished her sentence. In contrast, conversations are carried out with much less apparent excitement and emotion in neutral cultures. Information tends to be given objectively, and if emotions and feelings are part of the conversation, they tend to be described rather than acted out.

How you behave in a new culture can certainly affect how comfortable the host nationals feel being around you. It will pay dividends if you are sensitive to what is perceived as "normal" behavior and take your cues accordingly. If you are usually very expressive, you may need to tone down your normal style a little until the locals get to know you better. Otherwise, you may be viewed as overemotional, lacking self-control, and, in a business context, unprofessional.

On the other hand, if you are normally very neutral, you may need to signal things like appreciation, thanks, acceptance, pleasure, and so forth more overtly than usual, or those around you may feel that you are unhappy, in disagreement, or unsure of something. They may read your neutral response as discomfort or disapproval on your part.

Once again, look down the following lists and figure out which side describes your own culture most accurately. Then identify which side, on balance, appeals to you the most.

Neutral	*Emotional*
• It is not very easy to read people's emotional states from their facial expressions.	• People openly display what they are thinking or feeling.
• Remaining calm and in control of yourself will earn you the respect of others.	• Being able to express a wide range of emotions is an essential social skill.
• Understatement is admired.	• Eloquence and emotional hyperbole are admired.
• Sometimes emotions that have been so far restrained can erupt without warning.	• Emotions are expressed as they arise with little or no attempt to contain them.

Countries that scored higher on the emotional end of the continuum include Kuwait, Egypt, Spain, Cuba, Saudi Arabia, Venezuela, and Russia. Countries that scored toward the neutral end of the continuum include Japan, Poland, New Zealand, Hong Kong, Austria, China, and Indonesia.

If you are traveling from one culture to another, the key is to establish as quickly as possible what is considered normal behavior in the showing of emotion. Rather than trying to imitate local behavior, make more subtle adjustments in your own normal behavior. Think of the brightness control on a television where you can turn it up or down gradually until it looks right. If you are empathetic, you will tend to do this automatically, in much the same way that visitors from the West in Japan often find themselves automatically bowing in response when someone bows to them. Minor adjustments, at least during your early days in the culture, will feel more comfortable and congruent to you. They will also send a message to the host nationals that you are making an effort to connect with them and want them to feel comfortable around you.

Levels of Involvement

This dimension is about how we separate the different aspects of our lives. In some cultures it is normal to keep the various areas of life separate; for example, to separate work life from private life. Casual acquaintances can be made easily both inside and outside of work without any commitment on either side.

These cultures are sometimes described as being *specific* because relationships can be formed that remain specific to the context in which they were made and do not necessarily develop outside of that context. For example, you might meet and play tennis with someone every week, but the friendship never extends beyond the tennis court. Specific cultures tend to be frank and transparent. Casual conversations are relaxed, informal, and friendly. Personal information may be supplied even though not requested. People relate to each other directly, sometimes with a precision bordering on bluntness.

In other cultures, however, a person's work, social, and private life overlap and are intertwined. If you are a boss at the office, then you carry some of that authority with you into your social life as well. These cultures are sometimes described as being *diffuse* because once you have formed a relationship with someone, the relationship is not considered specific to the particular context in which it was formed. Once someone is considered a friend, then that person is a friend in every sense of the word and is entitled to all the commitments and obligations that friendship in the culture entails. Clearly, letting someone into your private life in a diffuse culture is not a light commitment, so usually there are social strategies such as formality, reserve, politeness, and indirectness that enable you to keep someone at arm's length until you have time to get to know her.

As before, compare the following lists and determine which side best describes your own culture and which description appeals to you the most.

Specific	*Diffuse*
• People generally appear relaxed when meeting someone for the first time.	• People are reserved when meeting for the first time.
• Communication is direct and informal.	• Communication is indirect and formal.
• Initially relationships are friendly.	• Initially relationships are polite.
• Relationships can be formed quickly and without high commitment.	• Relationships are only formed over time and invariably involve high commitment.

Diffuse cultures include China, Kuwait, Venezuela, Germany, Singapore, Indonesia, Egypt, and South Korea. Specific cultures include Sweden, the United States, Denmark, Switzerland, the Netherlands, and Australia.

This dimension also explains a prime source of misunderstanding between people from different cultures. If you are traveling from a specific culture to a diffuse culture, you may initially be disappointed at what seems like the unfriendly nature of the hosts. It seems almost impossible to get to know anyone beyond the superficial politeness and the excessive ritual and formality that appear to characterize all relationships. You may even come away from a conversation with the impression that the other person was evasive, overly tactful, and ambiguous. It is as if you are being deliberately kept at arm's length (which in fact you are) until people consider they know you well enough to form a relationship with you. Persevere, however, and you could have a friend for life.

If you are from a diffuse culture and travel to a specific culture, you may run the risk of mistaking the friendliness of your host for actual friendship, which it is not. An exchange of personal information, the discovery of mutual common ground, and the invited use of some aspects of your host's property, such as a car, could easily lead you to believe that your host now regards you as a close friend. As a result, you may decide to reciprocate your own commitment of friendship, only later to find that, although you offered your friendship without reserve, the host had in fact only offered you access to his property, which was open to all casual acquaintances.

Locus of Control

This dimension is concerned with how people relate to their natural environment and how much control they believe they have over events that influence them and their behavior. This dimension was first developed by Julian Rotter (1954, 1982). *Locus of control* is the term he used to describe the ways in which an individual attributes responsibility for events that take place—to factors within himself and within his control (*internal*) as well as to factors outside his control (*external*). In simple terms, if a person's locus of control is internal, he will assume that he is in control of his own destiny, have a strong sense of responsibility, and believe that he can influence or control what happens to him.

On the other hand, if a person has a high external locus of control, he will often blame others or some external force beyond his control (such as fate, powerful others, chance, or God) for what happens to him. In effect he believes that he is not in control of what happens to him.

Further research by Patricia Gurin, Gerald Gurin, Rosina C. Lao, and Muriel Beattie (1969) found that internal control was not a single dimension but was in fact multidimensional and based on two key distinctions.

1. The first was the distinction that some may feel they are in control of their own life, but they believe most other people are not.
2. The second distinction, which they found was more likely for poor people or victims of discrimination, was that some people feel that other people control their own destinies, but they themselves do not.

Other factors and circumstances may also influence an individual's locus of control. Immigrants, for example, may feel their locus of control is shifting from internal to external as they try to adjust to their new environment. In collectivistic cultures and cultures with a high power distance, individuals may find that the control exercised by society, the group, or the extended family has more meaning for them than their own individual control.

At a national level, cultures generally lean more toward one locus or the other. If a culture tends to have an internal locus, it will view nature as a force to be controlled in much the same way that a complex machine may be controlled once the operator has gained an understanding of its various parts. If a culture leans more toward the external locus of control, then it will accept that it is better for humankind to work in harmony with nature rather than try to control and work against it.

For example, one of the biggest outlays of money for subsistence farmers in East Africa is the purchase of seed for the next crop. The timing of the planting is critical. However, even with a lifetime of experience, a capricious weather system can undermine the most experienced farmer's judgment. A short spell of early rain, enough to start the seeds growing, followed by two or three weeks of relentless sunshine can destroy a family's uninsured investment before the main rains properly begin, a stressful situation for anyone. I was always impressed, and even amazed, by the stoic way the farmers I knew in Kenya seemed to cope with such a disaster. They accepted the existence of forces beyond their control. They still made the best decisions they could and worked hard to ensure a successful result, but they knew when to abdicate responsibility for factors out of their control and, as a result, they slept at night.

I often tried to imagine how Europeans or Americans with a high degree of internal control would cope in a similar situation, knowing there was no insurance policy to bail them out. Would they blame themselves for planting the seeds too early? Would they remain in a state of stressed alertness for the entire agricultural year, right from the planting to the harvest, even if the rains eventually came on time and everything went according to plan? A belief in the hand of God, or fate, or destiny can sometimes be an effective antidote to the guilt, blame, and stress brought about by failing to achieve some internally set standard of personal performance.

Compare the following two lists and first decide which side describes your own values; then consider which side most closely describes your own culture.

External Locus
- People have a strong belief in destiny and fate.
- There is a strong religious influence over life in general.
- People are comfortable with natural cyclical changes.
- People accept that the force of nature cannot be controlled.

Internal Locus
- People focus on themselves and self-improvement.
- Self-help books are widely available and sell well.
- People have a strong drive to control the external environment.
- People feel frustration and discomfort when natural elements display their power.

Cultures that are considered to have an internal locus of control include Norway, the United States, Australia, Canada, New Zealand, the United Kingdom, and Israel. Cultures that are considered to have an external locus of control include Venezuela, China, Russia, Egypt, and Saudi Arabia.

Intercultural travelers need to have a balance between internal and external control. On the one hand, they will need to gather information and be flexible in their approach to obtaining it. They also need a certain level of confidence in their ability to look after themselves and function in a new environment. On the other hand, they need to accept that there are many aspects to living in a new culture over which they have no influence at all, such as delays, red tape, political change, different cultural values, and acts of nature. Believing you can control the uncontrollable and attempting to do so may seem to some a quixotic, even admirable, attitude to have. It is also a quick and sure route to frustration, disillusionment, and self-imposed pressure. I suspect there may even be a correlation between the Type A and Type B personality classifications discussed in Chapter 4 and the way in which internal locus of control is experienced and expressed by an individual. Clearly there is a balance to reach. The sojourner who leaves too much to fate, destiny, and others will not catch many trains, buses, or planes, nor will she be as likely to initiate the sort of learning and change that is driven by an inner need to have some control over the situations that all travelers eventually face.

The old adage that a person should pray for the courage to change the things that can be changed, the grace to accept what cannot be changed, and the wisdom to know the difference is particularly relevant in considering this dimension.

Time Orientation

Edward T. Hall (1959), in his book *The Silent Language,* describes two ways of structuring time: *monochronic* and *polychronic.* People from cultures that operate in monochronic time tend to focus sequentially on one activity at a time. They compartmentalize time schedules to serve their own needs and separate task-oriented time from social time. Plans are drawn up and are generally followed; appointments are made and kept. Schedules often take precedence over relationships. In short, time is something to be measured, controlled, and apportioned to meet planned objectives.

In contrast, people in cultures oriented toward polychronic time are comfortable juggling a variety of tasks at the same time. They tend to put more emphasis on relationships and completing transactions as opposed to meeting schedule deadlines. The importance and significance of the relationship will dictate how rigidly the schedule is followed, or if it is followed at all. For polychronic people, time spent socializing is seldom experienced as "wasted."

Monochronic	*Polychronic*
• Tasks tend to be completed sequentially one at a time.	• Many tasks running at the same time.
• It is important that meetings start on time and run to schedule. The schedule takes precedence over the people concerned.	• The agreed schedule or timetable is subordinate to the relationships involved and the purpose of the meeting.
• There is a belief that time can be controlled.	• Time cannot be controlled; it is merely a means of orienting oneself.

According to Hall (1983), polychronic time cultures include Latin America, the Middle East, Japan, and France, while Northern Europe, North America (Canada and the United States), and Germany are examples of monochronic time cultures.

Sojourners from a monochronic culture often find that traveling in a culture where polychronic time is the norm tests their patience. For example, it might annoy you to be served by someone in an office, shop, or restaurant who is also carrying out numerous other tasks at the same time, including serving people who clearly entered after you. You feel as if you do not have their full attention and that they are not paying you due respect as a customer.

In fact, in monochronic cultures, customer service training courses often emphasize that the person standing in front you should have your full attention, and that in most instances you should ignore all other distractions such as telephone calls until you have dealt with his needs. This, of course, is the quintessential sequential approach of the monochronic culture. In polychronic cultures, schedules often flex to accommodate the needs of the moment. Travelers from a monochronic culture may be alternately dismayed as they wait and wait for an earlier appointment to finish, and then delighted at the unaccustomed time and personal attention they finally receive.

The traveler from a polychronic culture can likewise be frustrated in a monochronic culture. You arrive unexpectedly at the office of a colleague with whom you believed you had a good business relationship, only to find yourself clearly regarded as an inconvenience. Furthermore, to add insult to injury, you eventually realize your presence is not enough to divert your colleague, even momentarily, from his planned schedule. He has no time to even greet you, let alone break for a brief, informal meeting. To people operating on polychromic time, especially galling are those times when they have been away for a week or so or have recently experienced a notable event such as a daughter's wedding. These things merit some immediate sharing and comment. Even if work is pressing, being told to defer their personal news to a quieter time appears not only cold and unfriendly, but also rude.

Communication Style

Whole books have been written on the subject of communication styles, so this short section can provide only a brief introduction to this fascinating subject. Communication styles vary from culture to culture, and often they vary as a function of one of the dimensions we covered earlier—individualism and collectivism. Edward Hall (1976, 1983) describes low- and high-context communication. In a low-context culture, most of the information in a conversation is contained in the words used. Directness, clarity, and a lack of ambiguity in the message are goals to aim for and applaud in others. To someone from a high-context culture, having instructions spelled out in such fine detail may make a person feel that she is being spoken to like a child.

In high-context cultures, most of the information is either given in the physical context or is already known to both people. Thus, very little is actually made explicit in the language of the message. Different styles of communication develop in line with culture, and high-context/low-context cultures, in particular, are correlated closely with the cultural dimension of individualism and collectivism.

In low-context, individualistic cultures, it is important that the speaker transfer the message as precisely as possible. As a result, great emphasis is placed on what needs to be said and the best and most effective way to say it. Precision and clarity are the goal. Ambiguity is usually perceived as something to avoid if possible.

In high-context cultures, apart from the message being conveyed, it is important to take into account the nature of the relationship that exists between the parties who are communicating and to ensure that the relationship is not damaged. As a result, communication in high-context cultures requires an understanding of interpersonal relationships. In this cultural context, use of direct language carries a greater risk that the speaker will inadvertently confront, challenge, embarrass, and subsequently cause loss of face to those at the receiving end of his communication. Therefore, words or phrases that usually pose such a threat tend to be used sparingly or not at all—words such as *no, why, won't,* and *can't.* An indirect style of communication in a collectivist culture is therefore more able to meet a person's need to maintain relationships in harmony. In addition, the common understandings that exist in collectivist societies help facilitate this communication style. There is an unspoken understanding and expectation that the listener in the conversation will take in all the pieces of information supplied by the speaker while at the same time understanding that the information supplied does not in itself contain the key message but merely provides a surround to it. Correctly deducing this last, unsupplied piece of information is the role of the listener. For this communication style to work, a high level of empathetic ability is required from both the speaker, who needs to gauge how much or how little information is appropriate, and the listener, who has to work out from the context and body language surrounding the communication what the actual message is.

The level of adaptation that visitors have to make in a new culture (presuming they want to adapt) will depend on the difference between their own culture and the culture they are visiting. For those from high-context cultures arriving in low-context cultures, being expected to say exactly what they mean, even if it upsets or embarrasses someone else, could be seen as either liberating and refreshing or simply as a lack of respect for others. It can also be stressful in that there is constant threat that the visitor may "lose face" or embarrass someone else.

Those from a low-context, individualistic culture arriving in a high-context culture may experience the difference in communication style either as a more considerate, pleasant, and even nonthreatening way to communicate or as a frustrating, time-consuming way of avoiding giving any information at all. Travelers from low-context cultures often misunderstand the language of diplomatic refusal adopted in high-context cultures, and because they have not heard the word no they assume that the answer is yes, or at least maybe. As they subsequently repeat their requests, the high-context communicator feels increasingly cornered as once more she packages her no response in language that would be instantly recognized by her fellow citizens but not by the foreign visitors.

In certain circumstances sometimes even the use of spoken language itself is superfluous in high-context cultures. I remember dining with a party of six Japanese who all knew each other well. We were on a small island just off the coast of East Africa, where one of the six had been living for four years. The meal itself had taken some time to prepare and consisted of vegetables and locally caught crabs prepared according to a Japanese recipe. Earlier in the day one of the group had seen a tourist who at first sight he had presumed to be either Japanese or Korean and had invited him to join us for the meal. The visitor duly arrived just as the meal was about to begin, and we found out that he was in fact Canadian. His ancestral roots were in South Korea, from where his great-grandfather and great-grandmother had traveled to Canada many years before. I noticed that my six Japanese friends quickly settled into a contented silence communicating with each other via occasional smiles and nods. From time to time one of them would offer to fill another's glass or pass a plate containing some food to a diner at the other end of the room. Once the visitor's appetite had been assuaged, he looked around and began to appear uncomfortable with the silence. He started several lines of conversation with those on either side and across the mat from him, which soon trailed off due to the others' lack of sustained response to his questions. The Canadian had not picked up the silent communication that existed among those present. The silence, far from being uncomfortable to the Japanese, was itself an indication of the level of shared understanding between them. It emphasized their collective enjoyment of the moment.

Another aspect of communication style is the degree of formality. Some cultures pride themselves on the fact that everyone within the culture is treated as an equal (or at least should be). An informal style of communication supports this value, and this in turn helps further "level the playing field." The frequent and preferred use of a person's given name, as opposed to family name, promotes the feeling that people are in fact equal, and for reasons of experience or talent, some may be given authority over others in specific situations. This is not the case in cultures where social stability is maintained through social differences and where people expect and respect the differences and behave accordingly. To make the levels clear, different ways of saying the same thing may be developed that convey different levels of politeness and respect depending on the occasion and the person.

Linked to this communication style is the level of formality expected in dress code and the formation of ritual behavior that reduces the unpredictability of common interactions. For example, as mentioned earlier, the exchange of business cards in countries such as Japan and Korea provides necessary information regarding a person's status. Inexperience in another's language may make a high-context communicator appear blunt and direct even to a low-context communicator, who hopefully will realize that the speaker has been forced to fall back on his use of textbook language and that it is unlikely he is being intentionally rude.

Low Context	*High Context*
• Instructions are explicit and detailed.	• Instructions can leave out many details.
• Communication is based on what needs to be said and the best way to say it.	• Communication is based on the context in which the communication takes place.
• Communication often assumes no inside knowledge on the part of the listener.	• Communication assumes the listener has inside knowledge.

Low Context	*High Context*
• Good relationships tend to be assumed by the speaker or deemed irrelevant.	• Relationships and group harmony are constantly reinforced by the speaker.

Individualistic cultures such as the United States, Germany, Scandinavia, and Switzerland are seen as low context; most of the Asian cultures, including Japan, Korea, and China, are seen as high context.

Wherever you travel, you need to be alert to the way the host nationals are communicating with each other and be able to pick up something of the operating style from those cues: the use of gesture and body language, volume and tonality, physical space, touching, and eye contact. These will guide you in a way similar to how you probably learned during your first visit to a library, without being told, that loud conversation is not expected or welcome. Patience is crucial in discovering the most appropriate way to obtain the information you need in a new culture without appearing to insult the other person or derail a relationship that is still being formed.

Keep on Learning

There are many more dimensions that could have been mentioned, but the ones we have covered so far will give you a good framework from which to begin—and continue—building your knowledge. Seize opportunities to find out from people what their preferences are and what they feel is normal within their culture. Such inquiries, when made at an appropriate time and with genuine sincerity and some sensitivity, are almost always welcomed and responded to positively.

CHAPTER
SIX

Applying the Concepts

With the previous caveats on when, how, and how not to use cultural frameworks still in mind, let us look at how an understanding of different cultural values can help you anticipate and manage your own response to those differences.

From Models to Issues: A Closer Look at Values

First, however, it is important to be aware of your own values. We looked at a small sample of contrasting values at the start of this book in Figure 1-2. Taking these as a starting point, add more values from the dimensions we have just covered and any others as they occur to you. Try to identify those values that you hold particularly strongly. Then imagine a situation where you are in the minority holding those values. Now, imagine you are confronted daily by situations that challenge you to uphold and defend your values or to abandon, deny, or compromise them. What do you do? You may feel that you can reconcile the clash in values in a way that you are comfortable with and that does not entail confrontation with the locals. For example, the payment of money to minor officials to "encourage" them to carry out their official duties may hit one of your hot buttons. To local thinking, this is tolerated because it is seen as a perk of an otherwise poorly paid job. The locals, however, all understand that such payments are acceptable only as long as they are kept within an informal limit, which of course is not written down anywhere.

139

Imagine another scenario. Suppose you pride yourself on your personal drive and energy and find yourself in a country that is laid-back, where people always put off today what they can safely leave until tomorrow. How would you feel—frustrated at always having to swim against the local tide, and maybe even a little superior, too? Or would you be able to adapt in a way that would enable you to be part of the team and still retain your work ethic?

It is issues like these that are the real challenge for those who travel and work abroad. Often it is not easy to identify the cause of our restless unease or impatience; too much emotion can prevent a rational analysis of why we feel the way we do. Ancillary and often minor issues may be the ones that we react to most violently, while the deeper underlying problems remain unchallenged and unresolved.

One way of describing where values fit within the different layers of a national culture is to view culture as an onion (see Figure 6-1). The outer layer consists of those aspects of the culture immediately apparent to the newly arrived visitor, such as the architecture, dress, language, food, music, literature, and so on. This is the level that many people who have never lived abroad tend to associate with culture shock. If the differences are many and pronounced, then the experience is more shocking or stimulating, depending on the visitor's point of view. The pace at which the visitor is confronted

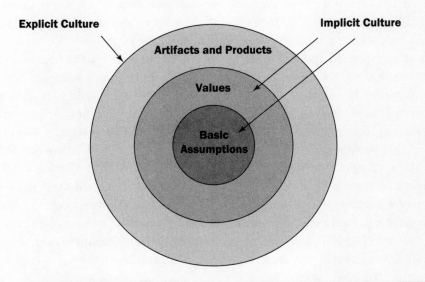

Figure 6-1   Layers of Culture

with the new stimuli can also affect adjustment. Too much, too fast, makes the new information difficult and tiring to assimilate, leading to a sort of "culture fatigue."

Deeper into the onion are those layers that are not immediately apparent to the outsider. The next layer consists of the norms and values that drive the differences in lifestyle and behavior displayed in the outer layer. You may attempt to imitate behavior you see without understanding the meaning behind it.

Values are broad preferences for one state of affairs over another. They dictate how people within a culture are expected to behave and what is considered "normal" and right. For example, you may personally want to behave differently—and actually do so—but if you want to fit into society and be considered normal, you have to conform. Cultural values impact and control most of what we do and how we do it—for example, how men relate to women, how close we stand, rituals around eating and mating, rules surrounding defecating, spitting, and so on. To operate outside of what is considered normal in your own culture is to invite ostracism.

The newly arrived visitor, keen to adapt, can mimic the outward behavior that he sees without being aware of its deeper significance and possibly also while omitting those telling nuances of behavior that his observations failed to pick up. Fortunately, the fact that he is trying his best to integrate is usually seen in enough of a positive light to more than counterbalance any gaffes he may unwittingly commit.

However, at other times visitors may find they are not prepared to sacrifice their own values in order to integrate and may in fact feel very strongly that the values of the host nationals are to be opposed rather than emulated. If this is the case, then integration becomes virtually impossible. The usual response to this situation is for the visitor to either leave or become entrenched in an expatriate clique that supports her values and views.

Let's return to the example of extra payment to officials. What the expatriate clique may decry as bribery and corruption the locals may see as an accepted way of doing business, at least as long as the payments fall within the unwritten, socially accepted limits, in much the same way that tipping and the corporate Christmas gift system works in the West. Again, what an expatriate clique may see as outright nepotism—for example, a situation where family members are always selected at job interviews—locals see as a pragmatic and sensible way to fill a vacancy. Family members who are currently employed stand to lose face if the successful candidate who is a relation does not perform to the required standard, and so will coach where necessary to make sure he performs adequately.

At the inner core of the onion is national common sense. It consists of those assumptions that are often taken as universal facts and seldom, if ever, questioned or challenged—unless of course, the holder ventures into a different culture that holds a different common sense. Edward T. Hall (1983) suggests that it is only by moving out of your own culture and into a new and unfamiliar one that you can truly appreciate this fact. Fons Trompenaars (1997, 23) gives the following advice for identifying a basic assumption: Ask for the reasoning behind the behavior. If the question provokes confusion or irritation, in much the same way that the question "Why do you breathe?" would, then the chances are you have hit on a basic assumption. For example, in East Africa you might ask why someone holds his forearm when shaking the hand of an elder of a family. The answer might be that it is to show respect. But if you were to then ask, "Why do you want to show respect?" the question would probably not only surprise locals but likely annoy them. For locals it is a basic assumption that you show appropriate respect to elders.

I remember when a local club in the north of England invited someone from abroad to build a traditional ceremonial structure in the town. One of the organizers later told me how he had been at his wits' end. For days the visitor just sat and contemplated. A band of local volunteers waited, ready to assist him with the construction, but eventually they began to drift away, disillusioned. The organizer felt that he was losing face and asked the visitor when he planned to start the construction. "When it's the right time" was the enigmatic response. Later the organizer arranged a lunch for the visitor and invited some local dignitaries to attend. "It's time to eat," the organizer said, interrupting the visitor's contemplative reverie. "How can it be time to eat when I am not hungry?" the visitor responded. Later, however, when the visitor finally did decide that it was the right time to build the structure, it went up very quickly, and a good time was had by all. The organizer later admitted that the visitor had forced him to reflect on his own assumptions about time and how he had begun to appreciate that he held different assumptions about time from the visitor. For the visitor time was plentiful, and the period spent in prior contemplation was in itself an integral part of the building of the structure. For the organizer, time was scarce and easily wasted.

If the host nationals have had little or no cross-cultural experience themselves, then there is a high possibility that they will be surprised at the sojourner's lack of understanding about even basic aspects of life, such as how to behave and accomplish tasks that they regard as universal common sense and that most children in their culture already know. Over a period of time, the traveler's sense that he is somehow continually falling short of local expectations and surprising people with his ignorance of the obvious is in itself galling. For the sojourner who is already stressed and, as a result, lacking his customary sense of humor, this can too easily appear as an unclimbable learning curve. This is the time when it is important to maintain a calm state, at least in public, and the techniques I covered earlier will help in this respect. We all acquire understanding of our own culture as we grow up. It is not formally taught to us. A newly arrived sojourner lacks this lifelong cultural induction and so does not yet know what he needs to know. And if the hosts have no prior experience of travelers and different cultures, they may initially assume a level of knowledge and understanding that the visitor simply does not have.

Attempting to predict which of your values are likely to clash, and in which country, is made more feasible by using the cultural dimensions we covered in Chapter 5. They will help you achieve the first stage of the three most important stages of cultural understanding:

1. Recognizing the cultural differences
2. Respecting the cultural differences
3. Managing the cultural differences

Recognizing the Cultural Differences

Recognizing and being able to separate behavior that is culturally driven from that which is driven by an individual's personality is not always easy. This is particularly true if the sojourner perceives little or no difference between her own culture and the one she is visiting. In such instances there is a danger that the traveler will attribute culturally driven behavior that she finds unappealing to individual personality and make no attempt to understand what is driving the behavior. Unfortunately for the sojourner, if it is culturally driven, she is likely to encounter the same behavior again and again for as long as she remains within that culture. The traveler may then start to form a strong, negative stereotypical view of the local population as a whole.

For example, suppose you were traveling from the United States to the United Kingdom for the first time with the assumption that you would encounter few if any cultural differences. If the first few Brits that you conversed with were reserved and indirect, you might find yourself believing that all Brits are reserved and indirect. Because you have not looked for cultural reasons behind the Brits' different style of communication, you have come to judge them negatively instead. You have assumed that Brits normally converse the same way you do, and the fact that they do not is therefore due to the personality of the people you have met, whom you have taken to be a representative sample of the British population.

On the other hand, travelers who visit cultures that are really quite different may be tempted to assume that all the behaviors they see are culturally driven because they have not yet reached the position of being able to distinguish what constitutes normal behavior within the new culture. In effect, they don't know what they don't know.

For example, when a sojourner first arrives in a new culture, she may be approached by someone who speaks her language and is very eager to act as her guide and introduce her to local businesses, where he assures her she will be able to buy everything she needs at the lowest prices. Her first impression, based on this individual, is that the local people are multilingual, outgoing, comfortable with strangers, and enterprising. In fact, the opposite may be a truer reflection of normal behavior within the culture. The individual who first approached her may have been motivated to do so because she was a stranger and could not know that he was considered a deviant among his own people. His behavior, which she has taken to be normal in the new culture, was in fact atypical.

Respecting the Cultural Differences

The second stage, respecting cultural differences, presupposes that the cultural traveler is able to recognize the cultural differences, or at least some of them. To be able to respect cultural differences means far more than just having awareness and an intellectual understanding of the differences. In common with all new learning, the learner has to first let go of some previous learning—in this case, her own culturally acquired "common sense"—before she can be open to new ways of thinking, perceiving, and behaving. Thus, being able to respect another culture often necessitates being able to recognize the shortcomings of one's own culture as well as accept the logic that drives the behavior, which may initially seem bizarre or even immoral.

One way to access this level of understanding is to identify situations in one's own life that mirror aspects of the other culture. For example, think back to the dilemma of the car and the pedestrian. In many cultures, the driver is considered to have some right to the friend's support and indeed would probably have received it. In other cultures, where universalism reigns, such support could easily be construed in a negative way, as not only illegal but also as dishonest and immoral. However, those universalists might well have adopted the same position as the particularists had the driver of the car been a husband, wife, mother, father, son, or daughter—in effect, they would have accessed a situation where their feelings and viewpoint matched the particularistic response. Another way of putting this is that travelers should try to find aspects of the host's culture within themselves.

Managing the Cultural Differences

The third stage is the reconciliation, or the managing, of cultural differences. Once a traveler is aware of the cultural differences and can respect them, the next step is to be able to handle cultural dilemmas without abandoning one's own cultural values and without asking the hosts to compromise their values either. Fons Trompenaars (1997, 199) suggests that people who abandon their cultural values become weakened and corrupt. When I was undergoing my country familiarization training in Kenya, one of the new volunteers persisted in walking around barefoot (despite the risk of ground parasites, snakes, scorpions, etc.). At mealtimes she insisted on eating her food with her bare hands, ignoring the knife and spoon supplied by our Kenyan hosts. She succeeded in upsetting virtually all the Kenyans on the farm, who saw her as being a naive and patronizing eccentric at best, and someone to mistrust and be suspicious of at worst. Clearly, attempting to abandon her own cultural upbringing and adopt what she perceived as the behaviors and values of the host culture was not a strategy that served her, or her hosts, well.

All cultures attach some importance to tradition and past learning, some more than others. Those travelers who suddenly want to cast off the accumulated cultural learning of a lifetime can only be viewed with suspicion and be seen as disrespectful. When we looked at the different layers of culture, we saw how simply imitating behavior you see around you will not in itself lead to an understanding of the cultural values driving the behavior. Those who take the additional step of recanting their own culture, for whatever reason, should understand how they might be perceived in the new culture. To many, they will be seen as not only denying their own cultural roots and heritage but also their personal upbringing, and what their parents and teachers did for them. In addition, they are also denying their new host culture any opportunity of benefiting from a two-way exchange of cultural information and learning. They are taking and not giving.

On the other hand, when the strengths of two or more cultures are retained and then combined in a way that adds value to each of them, this is a reconciling result.

Reconciling a Solution

One way of outlining the options in a situation and then working out how to manage the differences in order to reach a reconciliation is to chart the dilemma. Our awareness of cultural differences is usually most acute when we are faced with a problem or situation involving people from a different culture and where our values are challenged or in conflict. One approach is to draw two axes and to label each axis with one of the opposing viewpoints. This step usually reveals the dimension of cultural difference that applies to the dilemma, it also should stimulate you to view even emotionally charged dilemmas in a rational manner. Figure 6-2 presents several options for how you may resolve the dilemma.

As you can see, there are five main approaches to resolving a dilemma: (1) Compete by persuading or forcing the other party to adopt your view-

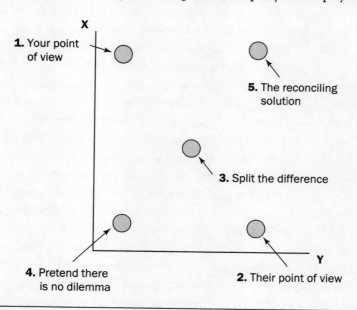

Figure 6-2   Charting a Dilemma

point, (2) Accommodate the viewpoint of the other party by abandoning your own viewpoint, (3) Compromise by splitting the difference, (4) Avoid the issue by pretending there is no dilemma, (5) Collaborate and agree on a win-win reconciling solution. This model (which, incidentally, appears to be identical to the Thomas Kilmann Conflict Mode Instrument) was developed by Kenneth W. Thomas and Ralph H. Kilmann (1974, 2002). This instrument enables the user to identify which of the above approaches is most likely to represent their own preferred behavior in conflict situations will make more sense if we use it to work through an actual dilemma.

A Case Study

When I worked as a development volunteer in Kenya, I was assigned to a farmers' cooperative society in a rural area. In comparison to most other farmers' cooperatives in Kenya at that time, the society was large—30,000 acres and 2,500 members—and composed of member settlement plots and a central farm that cultivated coffee, sisal, and citrus fruits as cash crops to help pay off the large debts the society had run up in previous years. Before my arrival, the society had received funding from Germany, supplied in two forms. Part of the funding came as a grant or gift; the rest, and greater part, was given as a low-interest loan that was routed through the Cooperative Bank of Kenya. Repayments on the loan were made to the bank.

A German overseas development agency had appointed a scheme manager to oversee the society and its use and deployment of the funding. He was to make sure that the necessary management, social infrastructures, and financial systems were in place to ensure the appropriate use of the funding in accordance with the wishes of the members and the various government ministries and that repayments on the loan would continue after his departure.

My function was to look after the interests of the members by working directly with their elected representatives—the chairman, deputy chairman, secretary, and six committee members. I was also expected to be a liaison between the German scheme manager, and his section, the central farm manager, and a settlement manager, who was newly appointed and who was charged with responsibility for the estate infrastructure such as roads, schools, water supplies, medical dispensaries, and so forth. The settlement manager was a local man who had been a committee member himself the previous year. The members' personal issues also fell under my responsibility, such as disputes between neighbors regarding the boundary line between their plots of land applications for employment on the central farm and any issues they wanted to bring to the attention of the chairman and committee.

My role as a development worker was to set up systems to support these people and to train a local counterpart to take over after my departure. In effect, my ultimate aim was to move the members toward being independent of outside people like me. Technically, I was responsible to the elected chairman and committee. I personally decided quite early in my posting that if I were ever presented with a situation where the interests of the chairman and the committee conflicted with those of the members they were representing, I would act in the best interests of the members.

Although I was not directly answerable to the scheme manager, I respected the fact that he had a greater understanding of how the various parts of the project fit together than anyone else involved. I also believed he acted from strong personal integrity, and I wanted to support him wherever possible. His role understandably meant that he was interested in ensuring that all costs were kept within budget and was prepared to apply pressure when he considered that any section was indulging in overspending.

The Dilemma

If any section was indulging in overt overspending, it was mine. In particular, whenever the committee members gathered, even if no work was done (in my colleagues' assessment), they often expected that a banquet would be provided. The scheme manager considered the whole ritual unnecessary and expensive. On the other hand, I could see that in a culture that placed such a high value on building relationships and on tradition, the banquets had a place and were clearly highly valued by the committee members. I also knew that the money funding the feasts belonged to the members as a whole, and I had already placed their interests above the individual or collective needs of the chairman and the committee members. So what was I to do? In the end I compromised by providing the committee members with a thin stew, a cut-price banquet. Looking back at the dimensions of cultural difference in the previous chapter, you will recognize that this dilemma clearly relates to the individualistic versus collectivist dimension in that the Kenyan culture is collectivist and concerned with the building and maintenance of relationships. The scheme manager, however, was approaching the issue from a more individualistic perspective where the task takes priority over any ceremonial relationship-building aspects of a job. If I chart my dilemma, the various positions would be as follows:

1. Cave in under pressure and follow the scheme manager's viewpoint.
2. Support the committee's relationship-building banquets.
3. Offer my compromise of a thin stew.
4. Do nothing.
5. Create a win-win solution to please all positions.

The recommended position is number five. A win-win transnational solution is reached, not through a domination of one culture over the other, but rather through a melding of the two cultures involved. The compromise position, number three, is therefore one of the worst positions to adopt (after number four, do nothing), since a compromise only half meets the needs of both sides while upsetting both sides as well.

On reflection, I can see that I could have used a lot more imagination in solving my dilemma and in doing so I might have provided a solution that was not only acceptable but of real benefit to all camps.

This is another key point—recognizing when you need to apply cultural understanding in order to resolve the problem or dilemma facing you. When I faced the banquet dilemma, I never saw myself as being in the role of a cultural synergizer. I certainly saw myself in the metaphorical position of being between a rock and a hard place and, though I knew what solution each party was looking for, I still viewed the problem in much the same way as I would have viewed it back home. I even adopted a somewhat lazy approach for that context as well, in that I took the line of least resistance—a compromise. I now try to actively look for opportunities where I can apply a broader and more creative thinking approach to dilemmas, both abroad and at home, because the results then tend to be more effective and the process itself more personally rewarding. Once you develop this as a habit and become more adept at it, you will be much more likely to pick up the signs that underlying cultural differences are the cause of a problem.

Now It's Your Turn

As a brief exercise, imagine that you had been appointed as my cross-cultural coach in Kenya. Try to work out what you could have advised me to do in order to reach an alternative win-win solution in place of my thin stew compromise.

To get you started, take the following approach. After charting the dilemma, ask yourself how it could be solved through consideration of either the task and rules or of the relationship. For a possible win-win solution to this case study, see page 179.

Chapter 5 and this chapter have looked at knowledge about cultural differences and ways of thinking that will help you understand and manage cultural differences you will undoubtedly meet as you cross cultural borders. The next chapter will focus on the personal challenges that you will face as a sojourner and how to anticipate and prepare for them.

Anticipate the Challenges

The first part of this book focused on you—what skills, knowledge, and traits can help you to be more effective at crossing cultural boundaries and what self-imposed barriers may hold you back. Part II has so far looked at important values orientations and conceptual frameworks that can be useful in recognizing, understanding, and managing cultural differences. This chapter focuses on the common challenges that sojourners and expatriates face. It aims to provide you with knowledge and useful models to help you understand the psychological stages of integrating into another culture and think through some of the key choices and challenges you will face. I suggest that you read the whole chapter first so you know what it contains and later refer to specific sections when they become relevant to you.

Although primarily aimed at those readers who are going to travel and live abroad for an extended period of time, this chapter is also useful to those who are not traveling themselves but who have social or business contact (perhaps even as a host) with people from abroad. This chapter will give you some insight into the process and challenges of living abroad, which apply equally to visitors to your country.

Prepare to Be Shocked

Most people have heard the expression *culture shock*. In fact, the anthropologist Kalvero Oberg was one of the first credited with using the term in the early fifties and in an article he published in 1959.

Usually culture shock is loaded with negative connotations, so one could be forgiven for assuming that it is something travelers suffer from but should always try to shake off as soon as possible. In many instances this may be true. It is also true that for many travelers, culture shock (which they prefer to think of as culture learning) is not negative at all: On the contrary, it is stimulating and exciting. In fact, it is one of the main reasons they travel to countries and cultures quite different from their own.

Even if the latter is the case for you, it is still useful to have an understanding of the factors that could influence your adjustment to a new culture. Culture shock is not simply about the initial impact of those differences you can see, hear, feel, and smell. For those who stay longer in a different culture and interact with locals, the differences that exist below the surface can be far more disorienting.

Challenges for the Expatriate Learner

When you travel, you leave behind your social support networks—family, friends, and work colleagues. It may take longer to build new networks than you expect. In group-oriented cultures, much will depend on how you present yourself and your ability to build relationships patiently. Technology, if it is available, will enable you to keep in touch with your contacts back home, whether by telephone, email, or even the postal system. Contacts back home can give support and advice, but they cannot provide direct support and resolve the specific local problems you may be struggling with, be they technical or cultural.

Technology also cannot take away the sense that you are on your own and ultimately have to rely on your own resourcefulness. This, in my opinion, is one of the most useful gifts of self-learning that travel can give.

In an earlier section in Chapter 1, "Travel—and Meet Yourself," I referred to how we come face to face with our own cultural programming when we travel. We are also forced to confront, in practical terms, our concept of ourselves. (See "Behavioral Flexibility" in Chapter 3.) How strong, how competent, and how likable are you? If, prior to traveling or living abroad, you tended to underestimate yourself, maybe had low self-esteem, then the acid test of surviving on your own resources in a foreign land can really drive home the message that you have far more resources than you ever believed. Some travelers have told me that, although they had felt restricted and even repressed back home, through travel, they felt liberated and able to become the person they always could and should have been. Their self-confidence and self-respect had been enhanced.

On the other hand, if your self-confidence has always exceeded your actual ability, travel can be a sobering experience. Being forced to confront your own limitations, to find yourself lacking in some competence you always took for granted that you had, can severely dent your self-esteem. Having the humility to accept the reality, and then to learn and grow from it, is the first step to a new self-confidence and self-respect that is built on inner strength rather than just a facade.

Those who define themselves by their role or job may find that they suffer from a sort of *role shock* when they live and work abroad. Role shock occurs when people find that they are not able to function with the same competence in a new culture as they did back home. They may need to learn special approaches and business rituals, make key contacts, or be part of alliances and networks in order to operate effectively. Building networks takes time and may require a completely new approach and therefore a set of interpersonal skills different from those that work back home. Because your role and your competence in it is central to your sense of identity and self-respect, it is not surprising that role shock can often hit harder than any other aspect of culture shock. Just imagine how it must feel for a newly arrived "expert" to realize that his knowledge and expertise is irrelevant in the new environment, and that his suggested plans and objectives are ignored. Far from being welcomed and feted by the local population, he seems to be perceived as little more than an inconvenient imposition. Role shock can have a profound impact. To compound the problem, expatriates often find themselves doing a different job from the one they signed up for.

Take time to monitor your own physical and mental state as you adapt to your new environment. Culture shock can easily lead to adjustment problems that cause stress. The symptoms of stress vary considerably from person to person. I have already described in detail the physiological processes driving the stress response in Chapter 4. Following are some of the more typical symptoms of being overstressed. I have grouped them into three categories: physical signs or symptoms, behavioral changes, and emotional changes.

Physical Signs or Symptoms
- Disrupted sleep patterns
- Exhaustion

- Digestive problems
- Muscular tension, aching shoulders and neck
- Frequent and/or severe headaches
- Diminished control of fine motor movements
- Susceptibility to minor ailments such as sties on the eyelids and other skin complaints
- Uncharacteristic weight fluctuations

Behavioral Changes
- Deterioration in appearance (dress and grooming)
- Longer hours at work
- Increased use of drugs and stimulants such as coffee and cigarettes or depressants such as alcohol and sleeping pills
- Out-of-character behavior with others: family, friends, work colleagues
- Erratic movements, tendency to be accident prone and clumsy

Emotional Changes
- General sense of anxiety
- Extreme loneliness and feelings of isolation
- Paranoia, believing that people are plotting against you
- Sudden bouts of tearfulness
- Negative perspective on everything
- Inability to concentrate
- Lessening of creativity

If you have a cluster of these symptoms or have just been feeling generally miserable and out of sorts for an extended period of time, then the first thing you should do is accept that something is upsetting you that needs to be addressed. This might sound obvious, but unfortunately many people experiencing stress refuse to acknowledge it and thus fail to take positive steps to deal with the issues confronting them. The expression "sticking your head in the sand" often applies.

Try to uncover the root cause of your symptoms; then at least you have something to focus your attention on, a problem to solve. Are you, for example, spending too much time berating yourself for how badly you handled a situation instead of appreciating how well things went overall? Go back to the section "Getting to the Source of Your Stress" in Chapter 4 and try asking yourself the questions listed there to see what is really driving your stress.

For example, one woman told me her stress levels had risen dramatically prior to moving overseas with her husband. Her husband had been offered the job of heading an overseas office. In order to join him she had given up her own job and had thrown herself into the premove preparations. The husband concentrated on work issues and gratefully left the logistics to his wife. Everything was going smoothly, at least as far as the planning was concerned, but she felt stressed and could not pinpoint the cause. That is, until she actually sat down and tried to get to the root of her stress. She eliminated possible causes, such as the stress caused by the change in their lifestyle even prior to the move, the loss of her job and contact with work colleagues, and her husband's lack of involvement in the planning of the move. The answer eventually came as she looked at the different ways in which they were both mentally preparing for the move. Her husband, who was more introverted, liked to think things through introspectively and to "recharge his batteries" by detaching himself from the day's problems and by playing games on his computer. She, on the other hand, was more extraverted and wanted to talk through issues regarding the posting with her husband. His stock response, that he "trusted her judgment," was read as an abdication of any responsibility for the planning. Once the husband realized the impact his behavior was having on his wife and got over his initial surprise, he quickly accepted how it had happened. Together they began to talk things through on a regular basis, and her feelings about the posting returned to ones of excitement rather than discomfort.

Try to break down seemingly insurmountable problems into smaller, solvable chunks and list them. Work through the list one by one, crossing off each issue as it is dealt with. The mere fact that you are doing something proactive, the steady accumulation of small victories coupled with the physical action of crossing off a visibly diminishing list of problems, is a powerful morale booster.

If you know someone who can offer support, do not refrain from approaching him or her informally. A local who can provide you with cultural insight is a good resource, though a local who understands something of your culture as well is ideal.

Just verbalizing how you feel to somebody else can often force you to look at things from a different perspective and to place issues within a more rational context—even if the other person's only response is to listen.

So far we have looked at the challenges that expatriates or sojourners face in general terms; let us now group the challenges into broad areas. You will in fact have to cope with three broad challenges in the attempt to deal with culture shock and move toward culture learning (Marx 1999).

Emotional

Mood swings, from euphoria to depression to contentment, are common during the adjustment process. Individuals who have a clear, consistent way of seeing meaning in life underpinned by core values—such as a vibrant curiosity to learn, an ability to live fully in the here and now, and a personal morality based on self-generated principles of justice, fairness, and respect for the dignity of individuals—will be able to put their emotional states into perspective within a broader context. Emotional resilience does not mean avoiding the down swings, but being able to manage and cope with them effectively.

Thinking

Thinking through and understanding cross-cultural dilemmas is a major challenge as you move from stereotyping to culturally effective thinking. The cultural models already described can help you in this area, but much will depend on your initial mindset. Are you open to new ideas? Are you secure enough to look beyond simplistic, black-and-white solutions and venture into areas of gray, where the challenge is not so much finding the answer to a dilemma but understanding why the solution works?

Social Skills and Identity

How effectively will you be able to interact with host nationals both in the work place and socially? Individuals who possess enhanced interpersonal skills are better equipped to bridge cultural differences. Genuine and sincere listening, where the listener really has an interest in what the speaker is saying as opposed to just wanting to make the right impression, is a priceless asset. In addition, the willingness to consciously be humble where appropriate will speed the bridge-building process.

Living abroad changes you as your basic assumptions and values are challenged and thereby altered. This could be described as a form of *identity crisis*. It is a crisis because the values and assumptions that you hold not only define how you perceive the world but also how you perceive yourself. For example, at the beginning of meetings and training courses, those in attendance are often invited to say something about themselves to tell the other members who they are. Many describe themselves by stating what is important to them and what beliefs they hold instead of stating their occupation. Your values and assumptions define what you think is important, what is right, and what you are prepared to defend. You may be placed in a culture where your values and assumptions on what constitutes commonsense are initially at odds with those of the host nationals. However, as you gradually grow to appreciate and even value your hosts' different perspective, you are also forced to reevaluate the assumptions and values that drove much of your previous behavior and on which your identity was partly based. Although this perceptual shift is often not an easy one to make, once made, it signifies real progress toward a more international outlook. If you are integrating well into a new culture, maybe even beginning to assimilate, then you have already adopted some new values and different ways of looking at life. For instance, if in your home culture you prided yourself on always speaking your mind and getting straight to the point, in your adopted culture you have perhaps learned to value harmony and to avoid unnecessary confrontation. To achieve harmony you have learned to express yourself in a different, more indirect way—a way that previously you would have considered "mealy mouthed" and even dishonest.

Clarify Your Aims and Purpose

Another factor that has a clear influence on culture shock is the amount of time you actually spend in the culture (weeks, months, or years). Linked closely to this are three additional factors: the purpose of your travel, what you aim to achieve, and how you involve yourself in the culture. The reason you are in the culture will have direct bearing on the type of interactions you will likely experience. Extended tourist, independent traveler, consular/diplomatic officer, visiting business traveler, expatriate staff—all have different objectives for being in the new culture and all have different agendas that they will follow to meet those objectives. I have lost count of the number of times I have heard expatriates and travelers at some point exclaim, "What am I doing here?"

If you are being posted abroad, you will be expected to achieve certain work objectives. I encourage you to set your own personal goals and objectives as well. Being clear in your own mind as to why you are going abroad, professionally and personally, and what you hope to achieve there will help you remain motivated and focused even when the going gets tough, as it undoubtedly will at times.

Having a clear overlying purpose for being where you are will also enable you to plan and prioritize and thus avoid drifting into the "activity trap." This is where you seem to be engaged in a continuous stream of activity (usually with other expats) that is without any clear purpose or benefit, and which you may not even enjoy. Being clear about your overriding purpose for being in a country is also an effective antidote for the obverse state—procrastination. The main fuels that fire procrastination are uncertainty and indecision. If there are difficult choices to make and the benefits of one over the other are unclear or even unknown, it is easy and tempting to just do nothing.

On a more positive note, having goals, or even some milestones of what you would like to achieve, gives you the opportunity to celebrate success along the way. Too often people plow relentlessly onward, stopping only to beat themselves up over some mistake or shortfall and never taking the time to pat themselves on the back for how good things really are or for successes as they occur. Unless you know what you want—and what it will look like once you've got it—it is sometimes very difficult to recognize small and even large successes when they occur. In short, if you can find a good excuse to celebrate and have a party, take it!

Yet another good reason for taking time to clarify your aims is connected to the section we will cover next—how you wish to involve yourself in the new culture. This largely depends on your own personality and interpersonal skills. Just as crucial, however, is how you decide, whether consciously or subconsciously, to relate to the host nationals. The key to answering this question is to know why you are going abroad in the first place. I do not mean a vague desire to travel or because it should be fun, because those reasons will not sustain you when things get really tough. What is required is a clear, unambiguous purpose that will act as a beacon and allow you to take your bearings, something that will give you a sense of direction even in the most turbulent of storms. To achieve this you need a systematic approach to clarifying your high-level, overriding purpose. The framework shown in Figure 7-1 will enable you to do just that.

This chart may look complicated at first glance, but in fact it is quite straightforward. The numbers in the corner of each quadrant indicate the order in which each of the quadrants should be completed.

Quadrant 1 (top right corner): Who is going to live abroad? Are you going abroad alone or are you going with a partner or your family?

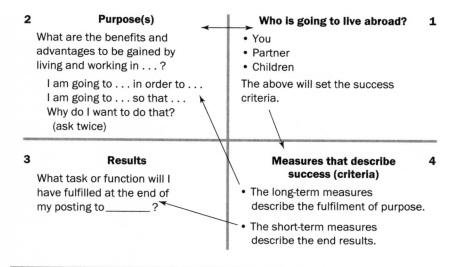

Figure 7-1   Clarify Your Aims

These are included because they may influence or have a connection to your responses in quadrants two and four.

Quadrant 2 (top left corner): What are the benefits and advantages to be gained from living in the country you are going to? This is the crucial part of the exercise, so take your time and work through your answer until you are sure you have got it right. The process is simply this: ask yourself the question, "Why am I going to . . . ?" and then complete the answer: "I am going to (insert country) in order to . . ."

This form of question is much more effective than using the word *because* ("I am going to because . . ."). *Because* tends to leave you where you started rather than clarifying your true purpose; for example, "I am going to Japan because I want to" or "I am going to Japan because it will be fun and a good experience."

Once you have generated an aim, the next step is to clarify the overarching purpose behind it. To do this, in relation to the purpose you have just identified, ask yourself, "Why do I want to do that?" In response to your answer, ask yourself the same question again: "And why do I want to do that?"

In Figure 7-1, I have indicated that you should ask yourself this question twice, but really that is just the minimum number of times you should put this question to yourself. Each time you ask yourself this question, you move up to a higher level of meaning by using the same principle as discussed in Chapter 4, in "Getting to the Source of Your Stress." In practice, keep asking the question until you reach the point where it is clear that you have reached the ultimate driving purpose; in other words, until the question produces the same response. When you have reached this point, move on to the next quadrant.

Quadrant 3 (bottom left corner): What task or function will you have fulfilled at the end of your sojourn? This requires a straightforward statement; for example:

I will have set up an efficient sales office in. . . .
I will have successfully completed the XYZ project.
I will have learned to speak and read Arabic.

Quadrant 4 (bottom right): Measures that describe success. This is where you list the criteria or measures that will let you know that you have fulfilled your purpose (from Quadrant 2) and achieved your end result (from Quadrant 3).

Let's work through an example. Imagine someone who has been chosen to head his organization's overseas sales office based in Paris. He is married but has no children. He works through the quadrants and writes the following answers.

Quadrant 1: Who is going to live abroad?
Me and my wife.

Quadrant 2: What are the benefits and advantages to be gained from living and working in Paris?
I am going to live and work in Paris in order to gain experience living and working internationally.
I want to gain international experience in order to fulfill a long-held ambition to work overseas and also to improve my promotion prospects.
I want promotion and the experience of living and working overseas so that my wife and I can increase our income and eventually afford to buy a house in the countryside and so that I can have the satisfaction of fulfilling my ambition.

Quadrant 3: What task or function will you have fulfilled at the end of your sojourn?

To have run an effective and efficient sales office in Paris.

To have built a network of French business contacts.

To have improved my spoken and written ability in the French language.

Quadrant 4: Measures that describe success (criteria).

Long-term

> We both complete the full duration of the posting and return home pleased that we accepted the posting.
>
> I get a promotion due to my work in Paris within twelve months of my return.

Short-term

> To receive a performance report highlighting my success in the Paris office at the end of the posting.
>
> To personally know a French business contact in every key sales area in France.
>
> To be able to converse freely in work and social situations and be able to read a French newspaper.

This example shows how the purpose behind going overseas can relate to goals that are not even about the posting itself. In this case it would also be worthwhile for the wife to clarify her aims and share them with her husband; then together they can determine how to achieve their separate goals before they set out.

When you get to Quadrant 4, remember that you can ensure well-thought-out objectives by using the universally well-regarded SMART checklist, which states five crucial attributes of objectives (measures):

S Specific	Objectives should be straightforward, unambiguous, clear, and understandable. *Ask yourself: What specifically do I want to achieve?*
M Measurable	How can objectives be measured—by quality, quantity, time, cost, or other resources? *Ask yourself: What will tell me and others that I have achieved this goal?*
A Achievable	Objectives should be challenging and stretching but not impossible. *Ask yourself: Is this really within my personal control?*

R Relevant — Is this really important and relevant to my future or well-being?

Ask yourself: Does this goal fit in with my other life and work goals?

T Time bound — You should have a time scale rather than an open book.

Ask yourself: When should I have completed this goal?

Once you have gone through this process and are clear about your purpose and what you aim to get from your experience abroad, it is possible to identify the most effective strategy to follow when you arrive in your new surroundings. The following section outlines the options open to you.

To Integrate or Not to Integrate: That Is the Question

The sojourner, expatriate, and diplomat all have a range of possible ways to live in the host culture. These can be summarized into the four outcomes shown in Figure 7-2.

1. *Integration:* Maintenance of own cultural identity, but with a desire for involvement and interaction with host culture.

Question 1

Is it considered to be of value to maintain your own cultural identity and characteristics?

	Yes	No
Question 2 Is it considered to be of value to build and maintain relationships with other groups? — **Yes**	Integration	Assimilation
No	Separation	Marginalization

Figure 7-2   Integration Strategies

Adapted from Berry (1980).

2. *Assimilation:* Loss of one's own cultural identity, absorbing oneself into host culture; may be voluntary or enforced.

3. *Separation:* Maintenance of own cultural identity with no substantial relationships with host culture. May or may not be enforced by the host culture or the nature of the sojourner's employment.

4. *Marginalization:* Loss of cultural identity while being denied membership into the host culture.

Integration

The goal of those travelers who answer yes to both questions in Figure 7-2 is integration. When you integrate, you gain the benefit of increased cross-cultural competence and a more in-depth knowledge of the host culture than with separation or marginalization.

Assimilation

Assimilation is a gradual process that takes place after many years of well-adjusted integration, where the sojourner is gradually absorbed into the host culture and eventually feels more at home there than in her original culture. If she has to uproot and move back to her original culture for political or work reasons, she will leave reluctantly and suffer badly from reverse, or reentry, culture shock.

Separation

For some people, separation may be a sensible option. For example, professional expatriates who have to relocate to new countries and cultures often soon become adept at sorting out the logistical aspects of making the transition from one location to another as smooth as possible. For those whose life career consists of moving from country to country on a regular basis, the integration strategy may not be a viable option. Putting down roots only to repeatedly pull them all up again is emotionally draining and stressful. My traveler type, the Self-Sufficient Sojourner, fits under this strategy.

A classic example of voluntary separation is the expatriate compound or clique. Expatriate compounds provide an oasis of familiar culture in a strange land. Sometimes travelers will even have met the other expatriates in a compound on a previous posting, making it more a renewal of old friendships than a first-time meeting. Separation may also be the preferred choice of some diplomatic staff who may feel that their position would be compromised if they made close friendships and allegiances with host nationals.

On the negative side, separation into expatriate cliques can prevent cultural learning from taking place, and if the clique contains a few of my traveler types such as the Sardonic Old Hand and the World-Weary Traveler, the group can quickly become a breeding ground for negative stereotyping. In closed societies like this, those who make a stand against the established "experts" and the peer pressure they engender may succeed if they have the respect of the group as a whole. On the other hand, they may experience marginalization even from the expatriate community.

Marginalization

Marginalization is not a strategy of choice; it is something that is done to you. When imposed by the host culture it is tantamount to ethnocide—destroying another culture. As such, marginalization is the antithesis of integration. History, up to and including the present day, is littered with examples of disadvantaged and disenfranchised groups forced to live on the periphery of society simply because of their "difference" or ethnicity. Marginalization is not always racially or ethnically driven. You can be marginalized because of your behavior. If your behavior does not conform to what is considered normal or you socialize with other marginalized individuals or groups, you may find yourself marginalized as well. Unfortunately, those who are having severe adjustment problems in a new culture can undergo emotional changes and adopt behavior that distances them from the very people who could give them support. In extreme forms, an inability to adjust to a new culture can influence a person's behavior in such a way that he effectively marginalizes himself.

The Cycle of Adjustment

The cycle of adjustment is often depicted as a U-curve charting stages of adjustment that travelers typically pass through before feeling settled in a new country (see Figure 7-3 for overall view of a basic U-curve). The model is well researched and most travelers can relate their own experience of adjustment to the various stages.

U-curves can easily mislead people into thinking they are mapping something that they are not. They are not mapping the stages people pass through as they acquire intercultural sensitivity and understanding (see "The Stages of Intercultural Sensitivity" later in this chapter). What they do map are the stages of adaptation people tend to experience when they enter a new cul-

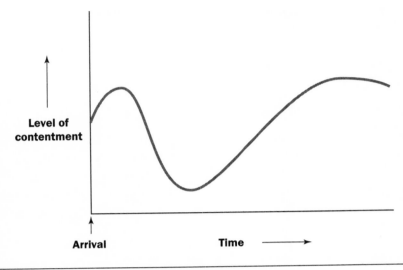

Figure 7-3   The Cycle of Adjustment

tural environment. I will give a brief overview of what the curve means and a description of the various stages of adaptation that make up the curve.

How low the curve dips and how high it rises are influenced by the differences between the travelers' culture and the one they are visiting. It is usually expected that it will take longer to adapt to those cultures that differ most from the travelers' own culture; for example, Westerners going east and vice versa. Research has also shown that when people travel to and adapt successfully to another culture that is markedly different from their own, their overall level of contentment and satisfaction is higher than if they had traveled to a more similar culture. In other words, the graph would initially dip lower, reflecting the greater demands and challenges being made on the traveler, but would then finish higher because of the high level of satisfaction and development obtained from having met the challenge.

The shape of the curves will also vary for different individuals. For those who find that they can adapt relatively quickly and easily, the curve will be shallower. For those who suffer from deep culture shock and never really manage to adapt at all, the curve will simply angle downward and run along the bottom of the graph. As described in the previous section on marginalization, some people may become so dysfunctional in the new culture that their behavior alienates them from not only the locals but other expatriates as well. Usually, however, the basic curve remains the same for most people, even those with extensive overseas experience. The adjustment cycle is essentially a learning curve that maps predictable phases.

Following is a more detailed description of the classic phases of the adjustment cycle. Your experience will likely mirror these phases to some extent.

Phase One: The First Rise in the Curve

The initial predeparture panic is over, and you have arrived safely. What follows is a period fueled by adrenaline. You experience exhilaration and high stimulation. So far, contact with the local population has been limited and superficial. This is often referred to as the "honeymoon" period of your sojourn and, just as in a real honeymoon, any problems that arise are tackled energetically and in good humor.

Phase Two: The Curve Starts to Slide Downward

Phase Two is the stage following the initial honeymoon period. The frustration of being bombarded with everyday issues requiring a solution different from the one that worked back home is starting to rise, and the effect is draining. Problems may include work relations, banking, shopping, cooking instructions on food packets in a different language, and the realization that despite the initial friendliness of the local population, you still feel like an outsider. Isolation sets in. In such a state of mind, almost a siege mentality, it is not easy to cultivate local friends. The tendency is to ask lots of questions about why things are done the way they are. Not surprisingly, those at the receiving end often sense some implied criticism in the questions.

The only people who seem to understand your problems and who can empathize with you are other expatriates and fellow countrymen. It can be quite reassuring to find that others share your frustration and annoyance at the local way of doing certain things. You may even encounter old caricature friends, the World-Weary Traveler and the Sardonic Old Hand, with a wealth of tales that conveniently support all your negative impressions about the host country. It seems almost therapeutic to slip into the sarcastic humor mode and blame the locals for all your current problems.

This phase is the most critical one, and the direction you take from this point on is determined by the integration strategy that you have chosen. For example, if you are a career expatriate who is due to move again soon, you may have chosen separation as your strategy because you consider integration unnecessary and do not want to put down roots only to pull them up again. However, even if you were clear that integration was the correct strategy for you, then at Phase Two it may seem very easy and tempting to gravitate toward the comforting sanctuary of the expatriate clique and socialize only with like-minded people. But beware—to do so only encourages the reinforcement of any negative stereotypes you have constructed, possibly to protect your own damaged ego or self-respect. If you want to adapt and integrate, getting stuck in this sort of trap will make it nearly impossible for you to do so. At worst, you will become more and more ill adapted and may suffer from psychological problems, stress, and even psychosomatic illnesses. At best, you will learn to operate within the culture but retain an arm's-length relationship with the host population for whom you have little respect (or knowledge). While you continue to build your store of evidence to support your negative stereotyping, you will probably, at the same time, hold a distorted and positive image of your own culture. Instead of sliding down this path, seek out other expatriates who seem to have adapted well and who have a positive attitude toward the host country. Obtain their perspective on the country and what they like or admire about it. Even those who choose separation as the most appropriate strategy for entering a culture can benefit from seeking a broad and balanced view of the host culture. They benefit because they become better informed and thus more operationally effective.

Phase Three: The Curve Starts to Rise

When you start to speak a little of the local language and to solve many of those problems that caused such frustration in the early stages, there is a sense of achievement. Your sense of humor returns and you start to look outward at your surroundings with more confidence. Friendship with locals, whether from work or social settings, will begin to give you an insight into the culture, and you will learn to adapt your behavior to fit in even better.

But be careful. During this phase it is very easy to imagine that you know more than you actually do, maybe even to consider yourself something of an expert, especially when showing around visitors who have recently arrived. You will probably have formed strong opinions about the host culture and its people by now, and you may enjoy sharing them with other expatriates. Deep down, if you are really honest with yourself, you might even feel a little superior to the locals. The danger at this phase is that by adopting the wrong attitude you get less out of your sojourn than you could. Feeling superior to the locals and, because of your local knowledge, perhaps feeling superior to your visitors as well, will not only make you less attractive to both parties but also makes it more difficult to continue learning about the culture. Once you think you are an "expert," the inquisitiveness required for cultural learning tends to be switched off.

Phase Four: The Curve Reaches Its Highest Point

In Phase Four you have gained a genuine appreciation of the local culture. You have moved past the surface of the visible behavior and into the realm of norms and values, maybe even to knowledge and acceptance of locally held basic assumptions. In addition to a deeper understanding and appreciation of these values and assumptions, you may also have adopted some of them for yourself, seeing them as better, or more appropriate, than those you previously held. For example, if you come from a culture that values achievement (live to work) and find yourself in a culture that separates work and social life and values leisure time (work to live), you may find that you grow to enjoy this different approach to life. To other expatriates, however, it may appear as though you have assimilated into the local culture and "gone bush." They may become quite critical of you.

What the Adjustment Cycle Does Not Tell Us

A weakness of the U-curve graph is that although it focuses on the travelers' feelings of well-being and competence at various phases of their sojourn leading up to full adjustment (integration), the graph could just as easily be referring to full adjustment into an expatriate clique (separation). As a result, U-curves of adjustment, though still useful, particularly to those going to live abroad for the first time, are not predictions of integration and intercultural development. Moreover, as we saw in Figure 7-2 (Integration Strategies), it is possible, for a number of reasons, to adapt to life in another country without actually integrating into that country. If you choose integration as the most appropriate strategy, the U-curve, though providing useful information about how you feel at various stages, does not give you a framework by which to track your integration into another culture, as I mentioned earlier in this chapter. Simply because you feel progressively more comfortable in a country does not necessarily mean that you are progressively learning about and integrating more into it as well. Fortunately, Milton Bennett (1993) has provided us with a six-stage model that focuses specifically on the developmental stages that lead to intercultural sensitivity.

The order of the stages and the stages themselves are based on extensive research by Bennett and other experts in the field as well as on Bennett's own considerable teaching and training experience.

The Stages of Intercultural Sensitivity

Bennett's model groups the six stages of intercultural development into ethnocentric and ethnorelative stages.

Ethnocentric Stages
1. Denial
2. Defense
3. Minimization

Ethnorelative Stages
4. Acceptance
5. Adaptation
6. Integration

Ethnocentric Stages

The first three stages of Bennett's model are referred to as ethnocentric stages. Ethnocentrism is an exaggerated tendency to think the characteristics of one's own culture are central, and superior to all other cultures. If you are operating from this viewpoint, then you will deal with cultural difference using one of the first three approaches: a denial of the differences, the adoption of a defensive strategy, or the minimization of the importance of the differences.

DENIAL. At the denial stage, a person is unable to recognize the existence of cultural differences. Indications that someone is at this stage are their use of stereotypes and their naive or ignorant observations. Because cultural differences abound, it is difficult for a person to continue to deny them or simply to believe that they only exist somewhere else. The only way a person can maintain this position is by adopting one of two strategies: isolation or separation. Isolation can be physical, such as a small town or village with few visitors coming in from outside, or perceptual, such as when the differences that do exist are denied. The second strategy is separation. This is where at the group level, physical, political, economic, or social barriers are erected to keep cultural differences at a distance, usually disadvantaging the minority group. At the individual level, separation may be seen as a slightly more advanced level of development than isolation because there is at least some level of acknowledgment of cultural difference, though the recognition may be both naive and denigrating. Maybe there is an element of denial in the mindset of the World-Weary Traveler in our earlier caricature.

DEFENSE. At this second stage a person can see cultural differences as threatening to his or her identity or security. Cultural differences are recognized but denigrated, and walls are built as protection against the threat. Indications that someone is at this stage of development are the use of negative stereotyping, "us versus them" thinking, and a worldview that sees one's own culture as superior and other cultures as still developing and catching up. Our traveler caricature of the Adviser adopts this position. Conversely, a person might hold up the new culture as superior while denigrating his or her own. This is just a reverse form of ethnocentrism. Our Please Like Me caricature is an example of someone who is probably operating either from this stage or the following stage of development.

MINIMIZATION. At the minimization stage, there is recognition of cultural differences but still only at a superficial level. Eating habits, greetings, and other customs are recognized, but the important cultural differences are played down or ignored. Indications that a person is at this stage are generalizing statements such as "We're all the same, really" and "They're just like us." These statements on the surface appear to be promoting some idealistic one-world picture. Our caricature Please Like Me has also adopted this minimizing approach. These statements appear superficially broad-minded, but what makes them ethnocentric is that the speakers deny, trivialize, or minimize others' unique cultural heritage while at the same time making the assumption that their own values and motivations are common to all humans. In other words, their culture is the benchmark against which other cultures are measured. This stage also represents the sojourner's last attempt to preserve a worldview as central.

Ethnorelative Stages

When you advance beyond the ethnocentric stages to the ethnorelative stages, you have crossed a major landmark in your development. You are no longer limited by an ethnocentric view of the world but accept that your view of culture is relative. You accept that one culture is not central or superior to any other. Ethnorelativism is based on the assumption that it is only possible to understand cultures relative to one another and that one culture's way of doing something is not better than another's but simply how the people within that culture prefer to do it. When you operate from an ethnorelative viewpoint, you no longer perceive cultural differences as threatening; you are in fact more likely to enjoy and actually seek them out. The ethnorelative stages begin with an acceptance of cultural differences, then progress to adaptation and then to the final stage of integration.

ACCEPTANCE. At the acceptance stage you both acknowledge cultural differences and respect them. Differences are no longer viewed as part of a defensive strategy but as alternative solutions to the way life can be organized. You accept that your perception of the world is shaped by your own cultural programming. Your acceptance of another culture is not just intellectual but emotional as well. You are able to respect and value cultural differences in both behavior and values without necessarily agreeing with or liking those differences. Although you may encounter behavior and values that you find personally offensive, you are still able to have a personal opinion about the differences that is not an ethnocentric evaluation.

ADAPTATION. At the adaptation stage of development, people have developed skills that enable them to communicate with those from other cultures. They can effectively empathize with those from other cultures, shift their frame of reference, and take on a different worldview while still maintaining their own. They are prepared to step outside of what is known and familiar.

People at this stage are characterized by a high level of communication skills and an ability to understand and be understood across cultural boundaries. They accept different cultural frames of reference and are usually viewed by others as multicultural. If their current intercultural development stems from the fact that they are bicultural, then one potential hurdle to developing further could be their ability to generalize their learning to date to cover adaptation into other different cultures.

Another factor that may prevent them from developing further may simply be the lack of motivation to do so. Indeed, there may be no practical reason for them to progress to the next stage. Their current level of ability and the high credibility they already enjoy because of it may serve their needs adequately. Even among those who want to continue developing their cultural sensitivity, at this stage it is possible to believe that there is no further stage of development. The stage of adaptation is sufficient for most cross-cultural contexts, but those who want to can still progress to the next stage of integration.

INTEGRATION. At this stage of development you can view a situation from different cultural perspectives and evaluate from a range of possible responses those that best apply to the issue and the cultural context you are in. At the integration stage you are not tied to any culture, even your own, and although you have the ability to become part of a new cultural context, you instead occupy a position that is not in any one culture but is on the margins of all cultures. From this position you can blend, integrate, and reconcile cultural differences and construct appropriate worldviews to meet the needs of the moment. Your identity and reality are also not derived from any single culture or group of cultures but are defined from within, by yourself. However, because you can view a situation from multiple perspectives and frames of reference, it is easy to be overwhelmed with the number of potential options presented to you. Development to this level can also bring with it a measure of discomfort brought about by the lack of a cultural identity. You have no single culture and set of behaviors to use as a guiding benchmark and none of the certainty enjoyed by others who steer their lives by cultural rules.

These are only brief descriptions of Bennett's six levels of intercultural sensitivity development. However, brief though they are, it should still be possible to get from them some idea of which stage you are at—and where you want to end up. The levels are not so much about what you can do but about transitions in how you think and feel about yourself, your own culture, other cultures, and those three aspects relative to one another. Bennett's model is useful, regardless of whether you travel or not. It can be used as a guide to gauge your own or others' level of cultural development and to help you understand why difficulties have arisen in cross-cultural interactions.

Part II of this book has been about looking outside of yourself to see what knowledge, skills, and traits will be helpful to you in another culture. Cultural frameworks will help you start to understand the different behaviors you will see in other cultures. With understanding there is a greater likelihood of acceptance and tolerance. You have also seen how it is possible to work through a clash in cultural values toward a win-win solution.

At any moment in time people from all around the world are preparing to travel and live abroad in another culture. You may be one of them. Yet despite a seemingly infinite range of different cultures, different people, and different circumstances, you all share some common challenges. These common challenges are, in the main, psychological ones. For example, knowing how crossing cultural borders affects you not only provides you with a forewarning, it also allows you to plan and to recognize the various stages as you pass through them. All expatriates and travelers have a reason for being where they are. The framework provided in Chapter 7 will enable you to make your objective explicit, which in turn will give you a greater sense of purpose and resolve to carry you through those days when the going is tough. It will also give you reason to celebrate when your objective is eventually achieved.

Finally, like all sojourners, you will choose how to position yourself within a new culture. The decision may not be made consciously, but the way you interact within the culture and the motivation you feel for being there will eventually lead you to follow a particular pattern of behavior. Be clear on how you want to position yourself. If your purpose for embarking on the sojourn includes learning more about the local culture, becoming more international in outlook, and increasing your intercultural sensitivity, then you will need to be aware of what attitudes and behaviors will separate you from the local population and prevent you from achieving your purpose. In addition, how will you monitor your progress in learning greater intercultural sensitivity? The frameworks provided in this chapter should help you with these goals.

Meet the Challenges:
Proactive Approaches

In the Introduction I stated, "If you have no desire to connect with those from other cultures at any level deeper than the minimum required to get by, then put this book down; it is not meant for you." I was referring to an authentic desire to build personal relations with host nationals for its own sake rather than to build relations just to meet some expediency such as a corporate or logistical objective. Edward T. Hall is quoted as saying, "I spent years trying to figure out how to select people to go overseas. This is the secret. You have to know how to make a friend. And that is it! If you can make friends and if you have a deep need to make friends, you will be successful. It's people who can make a friend, who have friends, who can do well overseas."

I hope the fact that you have read this far indicates that you do have a genuine desire to connect with those you meet from other cultures, and at a deeper level. I promised to define the key differentiators of an effective culture-crosser and suggest how the less successful sojourners could improve their effectiveness, and I also promised to those readers who really struggle in the area of cross-cultural interaction to describe how the Myers-Briggs Type Indicator could be used to help them identify areas they could then develop to improve their effectiveness.

"If you do not know yourself, then you will never get to know anyone else" is an old cliché, but it is certainly true of sojourners and other culture crossers. Successful sojourners are high on self-knowledge; they know their values, strengths, weaknesses, and expectations. Part I, "Looking In" (Chapters 1 to 4), is concerned with values, the self-imposed barriers that will hinder your cross-cultural effectiveness and development and the important cross-cultural traits that will take it forward. Chapter 4 provides you with tools to enhance greater self-awareness, areas for development and personal mastery. Part II, "Looking Out" (Chapters 5 to 7), is concerned with knowledge and conceptual frameworks that will help you understand cultural differences, how best to manage them, the challenges you can expect to face as a sojourner, and how best to anticipate, overcome, and learn from them. Using this "inside out" approach will equip you and help you to make the most of your own strengths and get the most out of your sojourn.

In closing, many cultural guidebooks give the traveler a prescriptive list of dos and don'ts. Those who like more rather than less direction appreciate such lists. There are also many, including myself, who prefer the opposite state of affairs—no lists at all. Thus, to end this book, I found myself facing a dilemma:

1. To provide direction and a dos and don'ts list.
2. To provide as little direction as possible with no list.

I finally decided to finish with some proactive ("do") suggestions of what the traveler should do and leave out the don'ts altogether. I will leave it for you, the reader, to decide if I have reached a win-win solution.

MAINTAIN YOUR SENSE OF HUMOR. Your ability to see the funny side of things and to laugh at yourself will be reassuring to you and those around you, and you will be more likely to enjoy your stay. Share your gaffes with close family and friends and even a close work colleague who can appreciate that you are really trying to fit in.

MAKE FRIENDS WITH HOST NATIONALS. This really is the best way of opening the window on the culture and of making your stay enjoyable and fulfilling. In doing so, you will also be extending your potential support network. Remember that your new friends may also be thinking the same—that you are now part of their support network. Refuse to be held back by the fear of making cultural gaffes. Usually you will be told early on in your sojourn about the serious taboos you must avoid at all costs, so what is left is likely to cause only mild embarrassment or provide a little welcome amusement for your hosts. If your intention is well meaning and sincere, you are more likely to be forgiven than castigated. If you tend to be nervous in social situations, especially when meeting strangers for the first time, study Chapter 4 and the section "Two Techniques for Controlling Your

Stress Response." The techniques do work, but often just knowing that you have the ability to control your stress response relaxes you to the extent that you don't need to.

DEVELOP AN INTEREST IN LOCAL CULTURE. Make a point of learning about those aspects of the local culture that fascinate you. This will give you a more positive insight into the local culture and enable you to start building bridges of common ground between you and the host nationals.

LOOK FOR THE LOGIC BEHIND LOCAL BEHAVIOR. As mentioned previously, all cultures originate in their own particular way in response to universal human problems. Culturally driven behavior has also evolved to meet different sets of circumstances. If you are uncomfortable with some of the new behaviors you are witnessing, one approach is to refer to the values orientations in Chapter 5—try to identify the dimension(s) that best explain the behavior and then to determine the logic behind the particular behavior you are uncomfortable with. Work out what advantage it gives the host nationals over the way you would have acted. Next ask yourself what it is about the behavior that makes you so uncomfortable. Refer back to the section on behavioral flexibility in Chapter 3 and ask yourself, "Does this issue provide a good excuse for me to try and extend my comfort zone?" Confronting the limitations of your own culture in this way is not easy to do, but it is the only way in which you can learn to adapt in a positive way. Remember, once you believe you know everything, you have stopped learning.

RETAIN YOUR CULTURAL IDENTITY. Do not worry that you will lose your own cultural heritage. You will not; rather, you will broaden your own perspective and become more international and cosmopolitan in your outlook. The ability to look at an issue from more than one cultural perspective should be regarded as a strength, not a weakness.

GIVE YOURSELF SOME TREATS. If homesickness sets in, give yourself some treats kept back for this purpose. These might be food or products you brought from home, or a short break from work to go on a picnic or see a show—anything that you think will give you a positive uplift. When you are feeling down, remember the cycle of adjustment discussed in Chapter 7. It shows that it is usual and normal to feel this way early in your sojourn. In fact, it is part of the learning process and precedes the next stage, where the curve moves upward and you feel a sense of accomplishment as you begin to make real progress in the new culture.

IF YOU FEEL STRESSED, CHECK FOR THE SOURCE. Try asking yourself the questions under the section "Getting to the Source of Your Stress" in Chapter 4 and use the approach to try and locate the source of your unease. It may in fact not be caused directly by the new culture at all but by some latent unresolved issue that being in the new culture has brought painfully to the surface.

BUILD ON SMALL PERSONAL VICTORIES AND SUCCESSFUL ENCOUNTERS. Do not waste time and make yourself feel worse by wallowing in self-pity when you have setbacks. Instead of reminding yourself how something could have been done better, tell yourself how good it actually was. Although the adjustment curve on the graph looks smooth and linear, in reality the cycle is a series of positive and negative phases. Imagine that the line on the graph has the same overall shape but looks more like a zigzag stitch.

For example, just when you think you have figured out a culture, an event occurs that throws all your certainty into doubt. I was reminded of this when I shared a house with two Japanese friends and a transient assortment of Europeans. One day a new housemate arrived from Scotland whose personality and behavior was quite different from all previous residents. One of my Japanese friends exclaimed to me in exasperation, "Why are you all so different!" Until the arrival of the newcomer, he had begun to imagine that he had a good understanding of typical Western behavior. The incoming Scot had broken his model yet again, and his adjustment curve took a little downward turn.

Anticipate these blips as normal. Learn from them and move on. Bear in mind that once you are settled, the problems tend not to come all at once, as previously imagined. Usually they present themselves as discrete, manageable packages that can be solved one by one in the normal course of life.

MOST OF ALL, ENJOY YOUR EXPERIENCES. Even for those of you traveling or posted to the more challenging areas of the world, the initial decision to make the journey or accept the assignment is often the hardest single hurdle to cross. I am sure that there are some people who regret going abroad, but I cannot remember when I last met one. Most travelers and expatriates look back on their sojourns with fondness and with some satisfaction. The greater the obstacles they overcame, the greater the satisfaction they are likely to feel. Travel not only broadens your outlook and your mind, it also allows you to build more confidence in your ability to meet the challenges that life in general can throw at you. Maybe the old adage "Travel is the best investment you can make in yourself" is true after all.

Happy landings.

A Possible Win-Win Approach for the Case Study

It is often jokingly said that hindsight is the world's most precise science. However, even with hindsight the correct solution to a cultural dilemma will always depend on the personal perspective and cultural background of the one who evaluates it. With that in mind I revisited my case study but aimed to work out an approach, rather than a solution. After some pondering I found myself with more questions than answers.

For example, could I have made better use of my good working relationship with the committee? What would have happened if I had worked through the relationship by making an appeal to the committee members and chairman to help me solve my dilemma of wanting to support them in their relationship-building banquets, while at the same time needing to control the members' funds and respect the scheme manager's need for some financial control?

Ideally, if they valued their relationship with me, they would have suggested a solution acceptable to themselves that would also have met my responsibilities to both the members and the scheme manager. Such an approach would have been more likely to produce a forward path that the committee could own and, as a consequence, be more likely to follow. The committee members themselves would also benefit from being presented with a different perspective. All parties did, after all, have an interest in the long-term financial health of the society.

Would this approach have taken me closer to a win-win solution than my thin stew? Yes, I personally think it would.

APPENDIX

A Review of Cross-Cultural Competencies

In Chapter 1, I said that I had researched what competencies others considered as prerequisites for the successful crossing of cultures. The following are by no means all the lists that I found, but they do give an idea of the range of sources I covered. It can be seen that many of them agree on at least one competency and most, on several.

The Quest for the International Manager: A Survey of Global Human Resource Strategies

In this Ashridge survey (Barham and Devine 1990), companies were asked to identify the most important characteristics needed by international managers. The significance of their replies is that, in contrast to the relatively lower priority assigned to "hard" or functional skills, four of the top six characteristics are "soft" skills emphasizing the human qualities involved in managing people from other cultures and the manager's ability to handle unfamiliar situations. One surprising aspect of this survey is that only 2 percent of respondents ranked awareness of their own cultural background as being among the five most important skills.

Key Characteristics of the International Manager

The figure in the second column is the percentage of respondents who ranked that characteristic as among the five most important.

1.	Strategic awareness (global view)	71
2.	Adaptability to new situations	67
3.	Sensitivity to different cultures	60
4.	Ability to work in international teams	56
5.	Language skills	46
6.	Understanding of international marketing	46
7.	Relationship skills	40
8.	International negotiating skills	38
9.	Self-reliance	27
10.	High task orientation	19
11.	Open, nonjudgmental personality	19
12.	Understanding of international finance	13
13.	Awareness of own cultural background	2

International Management Competencies

Drawing on a total of sixty interviews with managers in eight global businesses headquartered in Europe, the United States, and Southeast Asia, the authors classified the competencies into active or "doing" competencies and passive or "being" competencies (Barham and Wills 1992). The latter competencies represent those aspects that are less changeable, are difficult to see, and are located deeper inside the person. They concern the way that managers think and reason, the way they feel, and the beliefs and values that motivate them.

"Doing" Competencies

A multicountry manager performs a number of major roles:

- Champion of international strategy
- Cross-border coach and coordinator
- Intercultural mediator and change agent

"Being" Competencies

All these competencies are interlinked and mutually sustaining:

- Cognitive complexity (thinking)
- Emotional energy (feeling)
- Psychological maturity (values)

The International Manager: A Checklist of Ideal Attributes

• Conflict resolution skills	• Ability to resolve misunderstandings and diffuse culturally driven confrontations
• Ability to communicate	• Ability to overcome language barriers and connect with all strata of society
• Flexibility and openmindedness	• Ability to adapt and change and to spot trends and future directions
• Broad understanding of business needs	• Knowledge of how businesses work and differences in political structures, cultural practices, distribution systems, and so on
• Interest in and willingness to try new things	• Openmindedness and the strength to let go of the familiar and tested for the new and unproven
• Ability to cope with stress	• Physical and mental resilience to thrive on the myriad challenges of working abroad
• Tolerance for ambiguity	• Ability to function effectively without stress when many areas of knowledge are still undefined
• Language skills	• Genuine interest in and commitment to learning the local language
• Experience of living or working in other countries	• Previous cross-cultural experience and an interest in other cultures and in working abroad

Adapted from Green and Holbeche (1999).

Cultural Adaptability Index TMA's 360-Degree instrument

• Cultural flexibility	• The ability to adapt to new situations and teams, accept new ideas, and perform under difficult circumstances

• Cognitive agility	• Ability to think clearly on different levels simultaneously and perceive several dimensions in a situation
• Conscious humility	• Natural willingness to show appropriate deference and respect and the ability to communicate respect and empathy
• Cultural awareness	• Ability to assess the meaning of culturally determined behavior (in relation to one's own knowledge and perceptions)
• Contextual integrity	• Modification of normal working practices to accommodate a different ideology without contravening one's personal morality
• Connecting	• Acknowledgment of the value and practice of networking
• Cultural communication	• Enhanced interpersonal skills that adapt to cultural differences; listening skills
• Collaboration	• Effective team membership skills, ability to draw out the best from others
• Cultural synthesis	• Ability to create added value from culturally diverse inputs and reconcile cultural dilemmas in a positive and synergistic way

Developed by Terence Brake (1996) for TMA. 211 Piccadilly, London W1J 9HF, United Kingdom.

Main Areas of International Capability for Development Center Construction

1. **An open approach to contrasting cultures:** Proof of interest through travel or study in other business or geographic cultures; recognition of different or conflicting moral standards; an enquiring yet objectively analytical intellect.
2. **Individual motivation level:** Individual's true aspirations include to work cross-culturally in a way that is of benefit to the organization.

3. **Balance between open/closed behavior:** Independent, good judgment; recognition of host business unit culture and expectations.

4. **Ability to listen, analyze, persuade, motivate, and direct:** Provides comprehensive communication on a continuing basis; tries to achieve consensus (dependent on business unit culture) but has confidence to provide direction.

5. **Consistent yet responsive style:** Even temperament; provides recognizable, consistent role model in both adverse and favorable circumstances; recognizes and responds to significant changes, yet tolerates minor deviations.

6. **Creating teams; being player and leader:** Sensitive, balanced behavior; confidence to allow experts to lead; ability to contribute relevant knowlege as well as managerial skills; sustains team aims above those of the individual.

7. **Self-confident and decisive:** Able to operate when isolated, both by distance and host culture; independent intellect; confidence in corporate core values.

8. **Reliable:** Resilient; able to retain a sense of perspective.

9. **Being in control:** Establishes credibility; provides an effective influence (Perkins 1997).

Cross-Cultural Leadership Competencies

Relationship Management

1. **Change agent:** Receptive to new and different ways of doing things; mobilizes others to identify and implement desired changes.

2. **Community building:** Demonstrates a willingness and an ability to partner with others in forging reciprocal, interdependent relationships aimed at the achievement of shared business goals.

3. **Conflict management and negotiation:** Demonstrates both assertiveness and sensitivity in using conflict to generate constructive outcomes.

4. **Cross-cultural communication:** Demonstrates an ability to identify cultural differences and adapts his or her behavior to facilitate effective communication.

5. **Influence:** Demonstrates an ability to move others to action without reliance on positional authority or proximity.

Business Acumen

1. **Depth of field:** Demonstrates a willingness and an ability to switch perspectives between local and global functional and cross-functional needs and opportunities.
2. **Entrepreneurial spirit:** Demonstrates the initiative and courage to take calculated risks based on the identification and analysis of high-potential local and global business opportunities.
3. **Professional expertise:** Demonstrates a commitment to the ongoing development of his or her business knowledge and skills to world-class levels.
4. **Stakeholder orientation:** Demonstrates a willingness and an ability to balance the sometimes conflicting needs of stakeholders to achieve optimal results for the organization.
5. **Total organization astuteness:** Demonstrates insight into "how the business works" above and beyond his or her immediate area and seeks to use this knowledge to get things done within and among organizational units.

Personal Effectiveness

1. **Accountability:** Demonstrates a commitment to "owning" problems and takes responsibility within his or her sphere of influence for the achievement of business objectives.
2. **Curiosity and learning:** Demonstrates a willingness over time to seek out challenging new experiences and an openness to learn from them.
3. **Improvization:** Demonstrates adaptability to changing circumstances and an ability to generate creative responses that add value under conditions of high uncertainty.
4. **Maturity:** Demonstrates a strong and stable sense of self with a capacity for resilience when faced with crises and setbacks.
5. **Thinking agility:** Demonstrates a willingness and an ability to attack problems from multiple angles while maintaining a bias toward action (Brake 1997).

Earlier surveys carried out on the U.S. Peace Corps (Harris 1973), technical staff (Ruben and Kealey 1979), military personnel (Gudykunst, Hammer, and Wiseman 1977), and business personnel (Brislin et al. 1983) all agreed on the importance of the following qualities:

- Empathy
- Respect
- Interest in local culture
- Flexibility
- Tolerance
- Technical skill

In addition, for businesspeople, important factors included:

- Desire to go abroad
- Spouse's support

References

Adler, Robert. 2000. "Pigeonholed." *New Scientist, Vol. 167 No. 2258*. 30 September. Pages 38–41.

Alexander, Frederick M. 1985. *Constructive Conscious Control of the Individual*. London: Gollancz.

Allport, Gordon W. 1954, 1979. *The Nature of Prejudice*. New York: Perseus Books Group.

Argyris, Chris. 1990. *Overcoming Organizational Defenses*. Needham Heights, MA: Allyn & Bacon.

Barham, Kevin, and Marion Devine, Ashridge Management Research Group. 1990. "The Quest for the International Manager: A Survey of Global Human Resource Strategies." London: The Economist Intelligence Unit.

Barham, Kevin, and Stefan Wills, Ashridge Management Research Group. 1992. "Management Across Frontiers." London: The Economist Intelligence Unit.

Bennett, Milton J. 1993. "Towards Ethnorelativism: A Developmental Model of Intercultural Sensitivity." In *Education for the Intercultural Experience*, 2d ed., edited by R. Michael Paige. Yarmouth, ME: Intercultural Press.

Berry, John W. 1980. "Acculturation as Varieties of Adaptation." In *Acculturation: Theory, Models and Some New Findings*, edited by A. Padilla. Boulder, CO: Westview Press.

Brake, Terence. 1997. *The Global Leader: Critical Factors for Creating the World-Class Organization*. Chicago: Irwin Professional Publishing.

———. 1996. Cultural Adaptability Index. TMA 211, Piccadilly, London, W1J 9HF. United Kingdom.

Brennan, Richard. 1999. *Alexander Technique*. Boston: Element Books Limited.

Brislin, Richard W. 1981. *Cross-Cultural Encounters: Face to Face Interaction*. Needham Heights, MA: Allyn & Bacon.

Brislin, Richard W., K. Cushner, C. Cherrie, and M. Yong. 1986. *Intercultural Interactions: A Practical Guide.* Thousand Oaks, CA: Sage Publications.

Brown, R., and E. Lenneberg. 1965. "Studies in Linguistic Relativity." In *Basic Studies in Social Psychology,* edited by H. Proshansky and B. Seidenberg. New York: Holt, Rinehart, and Winston.

Buckingham, B., and C. Coffman. 2000. *First Break All the Rules: What the World's Greatest Managers Do Differently.* New York: Simon & Schuster Business Books.

Clarke, Kenneth E., and George A. Miller. 1970. *Psychology: The Behavioral and Social Science Survey.* Englewood Cliffs, NJ: Prentice-Hall.

Detweiler, Richard. 1980. "The Categorization of the Actions of People from Another Culture: A Conceptual Analysis and Behavioral Outcome." *International Journal of Intercultural Relations* 4, no. 3–4.

Friedman, Meyer, and Ray H. Rosenman. 1975. *Type A Behavior and Your Heart.* Greenwich, CT: Fawcett.

Goleman, Daniel. 1996. *Emotional Intelligence: Why It Can Matter More than IQ.* London: Bloomsbury Publishing Plc.

Green, Caroline, and Linda Holbeche. 1999. *Towards Global Leadership.* West Sussex, UK: The Roffey Park Management Institute.

Gudykunst, W. B., R. L. Wiseman, and M. Hammer. 1977. *Determinants of the Sojourner's Attitudinal Satisfaction.* New Brunswick, NJ: Communication Yearbook.

Gurin, Patricia, Gerald Gurin, Rosina C. Lao, and M. Muriel Beattie. 1969. "Internal-External Control in the Motivational Dynamics of Negro Youth." *Journal of Social Issues* 25.

Hall, Edward T. 1959. *The Silent Language.* New York: Anchor Press, Doubleday.

———. 1976. *Beyond Culture.* New York: Doubleday.

———. 1983. *The Dance of Life.* New York: Doubleday.

Hall, L. Michael. 2000. *Dragon Slaying: Dragons into Princes,* 2d ed. Clifton, CO: E.T. Publications.

Hall, L. Michael, and B. Belnap. 1999. *The Sourcebook of Magic: A Comprehensive Guide to the Technology of NLP.* Carmarthen, Wales, UK: Crown House Publishing Limited.

Harris, J. G. 1973. "A Science of the South Pacific: An Analysis of the Character Structure of the Peace Corps Volunteer." *American Psychologist* 28, 232–47.

Hausdorff, Jeffrey M., and Becca R. Levy. 2000. *Journal of Gerontology: Psychological Sciences.* 55, 205–13.

Hofstede, Geert. 1991. *Cultures and Organizations: Software of the Mind.* Maidenhead, Berkshire, UK: McGraw-Hill Europe.

———. 2001. *Culture's Consequences: International Differences in Work-related Values.* 2d ed. Thousand Oaks, CA: Sage Publications.

Kluckhohn, Florence, and Fred Strodtbeck. 1961. *Variations in Value Orientations.* New York: Row, Peterson.

Kohls, L. Robert. 2001. *Learning to Think Korean: A Guide to Living and Working in Korea.* Yarmouth, ME: Intercultural Press.

Kolb, David. 1984. *Experiential Learning: Experience as the Source of Learning and Development.* Englewood Cliffs, NJ: Prentice Hall.

Marx, Elisabeth. 1999. *Breaking Through Culture Shock.* London: Nicholas Brealey Publishing Limited.

Mehrabian, Albert. 1972. *Nonverbal Communication.* Chicago: Aldine-Atherton.

Morita, Akio. 1988. *Made in Japan.* Glasgow, UK: Fontana/Collins Paperbacks.

Myers, Isabel Briggs, with Peter B. Myers. 1993. *Gifts Differing: Understanding Personality Type.* Palo Alto, CA: Consulting Psychologists Press.

Novick, Noreen. 1979. In *The Nature of Prejudice* by Gordon Allport. New York: Perseus Book Group.

Quenk, Naomi L. 1993. *Beside Ourselves.* Palo Alto, CA: Davies-Black Publishing.

Oberg, Kalvero. 1959. "Culture Shock: Adjustment to New Cultural Environments." *Practical Anthropology* 7.

Ohmae, Kenichi. 1982. *The Mind of the Strategist: Business Planning for Competitive Advantage.* New York. The Penguin Business Library, Penguin, United Kingdom, by arrangement with McGraw-Hill Book Company.

Osterhout, Lee, M. Bersick, and J. McLaughlin. 1977. *Memory and Cognition* 25, 273–85.

Pearman, Roger R. and Sarah C. Albritton. 1997. *I'm Not Crazy, I'm Just Not You.* Palo Alto, CA: Davies-Black Publishing.

Perkins, Stephen J. 1997. *Internationalization: The People Dimension: Human Resource Strategies for Global Expansion.* London: Kogan Page.

Rotter, Julian B. 1954. *Social Learning and Clinical Psychology.* Englewood Cliffs, NJ: Prentice-Hall.

Rotter, Julian B. 1982. *The Development and Applications of Social Learning Theory: Selected Papers.* New York: Praeger.

Ruben, Brent D., and Daniel J. Kealey. 1979. "Behavioral Assessment of Communication Competency and the Prediction of Cross-Cultural Adaptation." *International Journal of Intercultural Relations* 1.

Schein, H. Edgar. 1985. *Organization Cultural and Leadership.* San Francisco: Jossey-Bass.

Schutz, William. 1966. *The Interpersonal Underworld.* Palo Alto, CA: Science & Behavior Books.

———. 1994. *Profound Simplicity.* 4th ed. Mill Hill, CA: Will Schutz Associates.

Seeman, M., and J. W. Evans. 1962. "Alienation and Learning in a Hospital Setting." *American Sociological Review* 27.

Senge, Peter. 1994. *The Fifth Discipline Fieldbook*. London: Nicholas Brealey Publishing Limited.

Stouffer, Samuel A., and Jackson Toby. 1951. "Role Conflict and Personality." *American Journal of Sociology*. 56. DOI: 10.1086/220785, 395–406.

Theroux, Paul. 1980. *The Old Patagonian Express*. New York: Penguin Group.

Thomas, Kenneth W., and Ralph H. Kilmann. *Thomas-Kilmann Conflict Mode Instrument*. Copyright 1974, 2002 by Xicom, Incorporated, which is a subsidiary of CPP Inc. The instrument is available from CPP Inc in the United States or OPP in the United Kingdom. Addresses are given at the end of the references.

Trompenaars, Fons, and Charles Hampden-Turner. 1997. *Riding the Waves of Culture*. 2 ed. London: Nicholas Brealey Publishing Limited.

———. 2000. *Building Cross-Cultural Competence*. New York: John Wiley & Sons.

Zimbardo, Philip G. 1970. "The Human Choice: Individuation, Reason, and Order Versus Deindividuation, Impulse, and Chaos." In *1969 Nebraska Symposium on Motivation*, edited by W. Arnold and D. Levine. Lincoln: University of Nebraska Press.

Contacts for the FIRO-B and Myers-Briggs Type Indicator Psychometrics and the Thomas-Kilmann Conflict Mode Instrument

U.K. and Europe

Oxford Psychologists Press Ltd.
Elsfield Hall
15–17 Elsfield Way
Oxford
OX2 8EP
Phone: 01865 404500
Fax: 01865 310368
www.opp.co.uk

United States

CPP Inc. (formerly Consulting Psychologists Press, Inc.)
3803 E. Bayshore Road
Palo Alto, CA 94303
Phone: 800-624-1765
www.cpp.com

Index